Marv Taking Charge: A Story of Bold Love and Courage is a notable memoir of Lois and Marv Roelofs as they travel the difficult "adventure" (as termed by Lois) from the diagnosis of a very aggressive form of lung cancer to Marv's death. Marv was midwifed from this life into life after—paraclete, *the coming alongside of*—by Lois, family, friends (far and near), and the home hospice team. Marv, Lois, and immediate family were sustained by their faith in God, developed over the many years of these relationships. This memoir serves as a guide for others to navigate the adventure from life into life after on their own terms—a valuable companion.

—Terrill L. Stumpf, RN, PhD, MDiv,
former director, Center for Whole Health,
Fourth Presbyterian Church, Chicago

Lois Roelofs has the heart of a healer, the soul of an artist, the voice of a balladeer. Her memoir is utterly rapturous—a long, sad, rejoicing, engrossing love story and a gift to all of us.

—Sandra Scofield,
author, *The Last Draft; Swim: Stories of the Sixties*

Lois Roelofs' husband wanted to die at home. This is a remarkable and inspirational story of a wife and family's commitment to honor Marv's wish. With the compassionate support of hospice staff, Lois and her family summoned the inner strength and grace to care for Marv at home until the end of his life. Hospice was the "lifeline" that provided ongoing comfort and reassurance for Marv, and especially for Lois as wife/nurse/caregiver.

—Jane Van De Velde, DNP, RN,
retired hospice nurse

As a counselor, I think Lois Roelofs is one of the best writers who delves deep into her personal experience to offer support and encouragement to readers going through difficult transitions and grieving.

—Ann T. Brody, MSW,
Certified Career and Life Coach

The story Lois Roelofs tells in this memoir of her husband's death is universal; after all, everyone's life ends. Still, no two stories are alike, and Roelofs' particulars are very much her own and their own. That she is a nurse means she follows his suffering thoughtfully, in ways few others can. Then again, their fifty-five years of marriage means her heart, her love, is also ever engaged. But the strengths of their souls, their mutual faith, provides the power that sees them both through. Her vigil will wear you out, but its exactness of her conviction will strengthen you for all of our journeys.

—James Calvin Schaap,
Emeritus Professor of English, Dordt University

A marriage well lived and a parting lovingly recorded in real time—that is the story of Lois and Marv's long and eventful life together. Retrospective memoirs often gloss over the hard parts, but Lois shares the struggles of honoring her husband's wishes to bypass futile treatment and watching the man she loves succumb to terminal cancer. This is a book that honors life even in the face of death.

—Carol J. Rottman, PhD,
teacher and author, *A Memoir of Parting*

A heart-wrenching story with lessons for family and professional caregivers on how to navigate the rocky road of terminal cancer. The words, "talk to my wife; she's a nurse" resonated with me, as does the rest of the book, since I lived the same experience: a nurse, yet a family member caring for my husband who had an untreatable cancer. Like Lois and Marv, my late husband and I counted on the support of friends and family and our hospice providers to help us get through the rough times. An important lesson both for families and healthcare providers is the importance of signing on to hospice early to benefit from all the help they provide.

—Karen Van Dyke Lamb, RN, DNP,
Gerontological Clinical Nurse Specialist

Marv
Taking Charge

A STORY OF
BOLD LOVE
AND COURAGE

by
LOIS HOITENGA ROELOFS

ISBN—13: 9781632695901
Library of Congress Control Number: 2023900383

Printed in the USA
2023—First Edition

31 30 29 28 27 26 25 24 23   10 9 8 7 6 5 4 3 2 1

AUTHOR'S NOTE

These stories are true, as recorded by me, my late husband Marv, our son Jon, and our daughter Kathleen. All names have been changed except for family; my friend Marianna Crane; Marv's publisher, Jeremy Brown; and my pastor, the Rev. Dr. David Halleen. The "Words from Marv" sections are adapted from the legacy book prepared for him in 2018 by Jeremy Brown at Throne Publishing Group, Sioux Falls, SD. Some of the original source material has been edited for a smoother story in this context.

Readers may connect with me by visiting my blog at loisroelofs. com.

CONTENTS

Dedicated to Marv Roelofs
My forever inspiration

KEY TO EMAIL CONTACTS

Throughout the book, I include emails that I sent to various friends and family members. See the list below.

Family

Kids and Grandkids:

- Our son Jon and his wife Sheri
- Their three grown children and their significant others: Kristin (Allan), Kyle (Kaileen), and Megan (Shane)
- Our daughter Kathleen and her husband Michael (who then share with their two young children, Madison and Jacob)

My Sisters: My remaining siblings out of four (one sister and one spouse—a sister-in-law)

Gals: My sisters, daughters, and adult granddaughters

Marv's Siblings: Marv's remaining siblings out of eight (six siblings and seven spouses)

Friends

Marianna: My friend for more than forty years, a nurse practitioner

Chicago Writing Friends: Two women from my long-term critique group

Chicago Nursing Friends: Two friends who walked alongside me during Marv's illness

You can have the other words—luck, coincidence, serendipity. I'll take grace. I don't know what it is exactly, but I'll take it.

—Mary Oliver

I do not at all understand the mystery of grace—only that it meets us where we are but does not leave us where it found us.

—Anne Lamott,
Traveling Mercies

INTRODUCTION

No man is an island, entire of itself; every man is a
piece of the continent, a part of the main.

—John Donne

As an English major in college, my husband Marv loved the writings of John Donne. In the quote above, Marv understood Donne to say that as human beings we are all connected and dependent on each other. He took that a step further to say that we are all responsible for those less fortunate than ourselves. Never losing that mindset, he started out after college as a juvenile probation officer in South Cook County in Chicago, then became a social worker in special education, and later started a health care reimbursement business benefitting children.

On January 3, 2018, when the events in this book began, Marv, at age 76, had just turned his business over to our daughter. He also ran our household, from finances to yard work to car maintenance. And, for nearly fifty of our fifty-five years of marriage, he had done and was still doing all the grocery shopping and cooking. Other wives envied me. One elderly neighbor even called me "The Queen."

Of course, I didn't know that the final days of our life together would give me material to write about for several years, eventually involving our two children Jon and Kathleen, their spouses Sheri and Michael, and our five grandchildren—three grown and two grade-schoolers. When we were hit with Marv's terminal diagnosis, I did what I always had done as a nurse—I began to document what was happening in our lives. I filled notebooks with my observations, used emails to update family and friends, and posted our ongoing story on my blog. The act of writing helped me to organize and sort through what was happening. Later, mulling over my mountains of documentation and deciding what to include and edit for this collection helped me to process our experience further—mine as caregiver, Marv's as patient.

This book is based on those notes, emails, and blog posts—perspectives ranging from private to public that I started writing one frigid day in January of 2018 when I had no idea what lay ahead. The book also includes perspectives from Marv and our children. I've edited the contents to shape a more compelling manuscript, but the dates and times are as recorded in the documentation.

My hope is that telling our story will help those of you who are walking with a loved one in the process of dying. Everyone's experience is different, but there will be commonalities in the emotions we feel and the tasks we must accomplish. I want you to know that it is possible, with appropriate resources, to help our loved ones die with dignity and respect—and to survive the time of caregiving ourselves.

PART I

A NEW REALITY

CHAPTER ONE

January 30, 2018

Not knowing when the pulmonologist was going to call, Marv decided that we would not wait around for his biopsy results. We left, as planned months earlier, on our winter road trip. Winters are brutal in South Dakota, and we were looking forward to meeting up with family and friends in much warmer Arizona.

Along the way, Marv wanted to see *Gunsmoke* memorabilia—he had listened to the show on the radio as a kid in the 1950s—in Dodge City, Kansas, so we took a moment on our second day to peruse pamphlets at the touristy Boot Hill Museum: Queen of the Cowtowns.

The trip had been good so far. The ice-rutted roads of South Dakota had gradually given way through Nebraska to the dry roads of Kansas. I'd been excited about this vacation. It was only our fourth road trip to the West. Usually, our road trips were to family members living within a few hundred miles. I loved the quiet time with Marv. He was never a chatterbox, so I absolutely loved having him belted in next to me, not able to escape. If I asked too many questions, he'd say, "That's enough for now," and chuckle. At times, he'd extend his right hand to me, and I'd know to scratch it lightly to keep him awake.

That day at the museum in Dodge City, we were happy, finally, to be in warm and sunny weather. Ordinarily, I'd have felt like this was a beautiful day of promise. But I wondered if Marv had insisted on leaving before his doctor's call because he worried it might not be possible later. So far, we'd avoided talking about "what if."

When we were finishing up at the pamphlet rack, about one in the afternoon, I heard Marv's phone jangle and nudged him. There were other tourists nearby, so he moved into a darkened corner to take the call. I remember him cupping his hand over his free ear to block out noise; I motioned him to follow me into the nearly silent, sunny outdoors. As we stood on the small wooden porch, I heard him say, "I'm not interested in treatment. Here, talk to my wife. She's a nurse. She'll understand what you're saying."

He stuck out his arm to hand me the phone. As I took it, I tried to read his expression. Nothing. Just as blank as if he'd been told the mail had come.

"I'm Lois, Marv's wife," I said, still watching him.

The pulmonologist spoke in a quiet hurried voice. "The biopsy showed lung cancer. Small cell. Your husband must start treatment right away. Chemo is the only option. This cancer is extremely aggressive. I don't think he realizes how serious this is. He may have only a few weeks."

I clutched the phone harder, trying to keep as much control of my own face as I could see Marv was doing with his. A few weeks? Only a few weeks to say farewell to a fifty-five-year marriage? The love of my life? Only a few weeks to get ready to go on without him?

CHAPTER TWO

Twenty-seven days earlier:
January 3, 2018

On an ordinary five-degree, wintry day in Sioux Falls, South Dakota, I headed to a coffee shop eager to start on my New Year's resolution to write every day. After picking up a decaf peppermint mocha, I weaved my way to a secluded corner table, shimmied a new spiral notebook out of my backpack, and set up my space to write.

I'd been looking forward to writing again. Two years earlier, Marv and I had moved from Chicago to Sioux Falls to be near our daughter and her family and, except for blogging about the move, I'd spent most my time getting acquainted with my new community. I'd left a writing group back in Chicago, though, and was only beginning to realize how much they kept me on track. Now I was determined to get it going on my own.

But as I settled in with my pen and took a sip of the mocha, my phone signaled a text: "When are you coming home?" From Marv.

He rarely texted me. I'd left him only a little bit ago. My heartbeat quickened as I texted back, "Why?"

"I'm having chest pain, and I want you to take me to the clinic."

This was not normal. For my seventy-six-year-old husband to be willing to go to a doctor, let alone asking for it, was unprecedented. "At Starbucks," I texted back. "On my way."

With my own heart verging on palpitations, I jammed my notebook back into my backpack, jerked on my coat, grabbed my mocha, and dashed out the door. Zipping my Beetle out of the parking lot, my mind raced. Uncertainty always made me default to the details of planning. Chest pain meant I would have to take Marv to the ER, though he would almost certainly argue for his doctor's office. As a retired nurse educator, I had taught patients and nursing students for years about appropriate interventions. It wasn't beyond Marv, though, to remind me that he was neither my patient nor my student.

But there he was, waiting for me in our driveway. When he lowered himself into my car, frown lines shouted his fear. In my calmest nursing tone, masking my escalating concern, I said, "Honey, a doctor's office is not set up to treat walk-ins. Chest pain is an emergency."

For once, he didn't argue. That alone told me a lot about what he was feeling.

As I drove up 229 to Cliff Avenue, I kept up that inner planning dialogue. I worried about Marv's inability to sit for long. *How will I keep him calm?* Once, I had told him that I was going to write a book about him and title it *He Can't Sit.* Marv was a bundle of energy. That wasn't good or bad, just fact. He attributed his high energy level to an internal motor that never quit. He'd warned our pastors he'd walk out if services lasted longer than an hour. He had told visitors to our home at the two-hour mark that it was time for them to leave. Along those lines, he did not do hospitalizations well—or any confinement, for that matter. He had insisted on early discharges more than once.

Heading north on Cliff, I glanced at him. No evidence of pain. No labored breathing. No change in coloring. So far, so good. When I pulled under the overhang of the hospital's emergency department, I braced myself; I would have to help Marv withstand a confinement once again.

Email

To: Marv's Siblings [Marv's remaining siblings of eight (six siblings and seven spouses)]

Need to let you know that Marv had chest pain radiating to his left arm this morning, starting at 9:00 a.m. I took him to ER. Nitroglycerin and aspirin relieved the pain. He had numerous tests, and doctors decided to admit him as they don't know for sure what's going on.

Kathleen [our daughter] was with us all day in the ER. She and I left around six in the evening. Marv had another chest pain episode at seven. Again, relieved by nitro.

I'll keep you informed about what we find out tomorrow. He may be transferred to the heart hospital for more testing. We appreciate your prayers.

January 5, 2018

Notes

I am relieved to be home. On my couch. My fibromyalgia pain is a 10 out of 10.

Last night was a nightmare. After being away from home for two days, Marv was told at the heart hospital he could leave after the last test. Kath and I were there with him all day, and I was waiting to take him home. Then a nurse came in and said he'd have to stay another three hours until the IV was finished and the dye from the last test had worked itself out of his system. His eyes darkened and jaw quivered as he announced, "I was told I could leave now." The nurse quietly said she was sorry he was misinformed.

Both Kath and I saw that the situation was going to escalate. Beyond tired, I quickly interjected, "Kath and I will get dinner. Call me when you're discharged. I'll pick you up." His posture in bed and facial lines had stiffened over the past two days. I needed a breather for my weary nerves. Nothing short of discharge was going to calm him, and I felt helpless in the face of his frustration.

As I left with Kathleen, she smiled at a nurse in the nurses' station and said, "Good luck." But she turned to me and was more reassuring. "Mom, they'll know how to handle him."

I was home less than an hour when Marv called. "Come get me. I'm discharged."

I threw on my down-filled, three-quarter coat, entered my frosty garage, and inched my way back in the dark over two miles of icy roads to the heart hospital. Marv was standing alone in the lobby, no nurse around. "When I saw you pull up," he said, "I told her she didn't need to stay."

I smiled and shook my head; I was not surprised. He'd always been like that.

Words from Marv

> Restlessness for me is nothing new. College was not an easy thing for me. Just like in grade school and high school, I had trouble sitting still and focusing in college. I never went to the library because if I did I would fall asleep immediately. If I wanted to study, it worked best for me to sit in the Commons, since there were all kinds of people walking around and talking. There was coffee in the Commons as well, and I could smoke, which

helped me relax. As long as I could smoke, drink coffee, and be surrounded by lots of noise and activity, then I could sit and study.

Email

To: My Sisters [my remaining siblings of four (one sister and one spouse—a sister-in-law)]

Marv and I just rehashed his last two days. First ER, then an overnight stay, then a heart hospital. We calculated he was asked the same history up to nine times. Kath said she had his history memorized. In my opinion, there is some room for improvement for hospitals communicating among themselves. If it goes in the computer the first time, it seems subsequent people could just verify with the patient. (Marv and I have had this discussion before!) Even the business office in the second hospital, both from Avera, one of the major medical systems here, had to take all our info again. And they did not have a correction I'd given to the general hospital the day before.

We're looking for the weather to warm up this weekend, maybe to the thirties. After this winter, that will seem positively hot. We still hope to leave in a few weeks for Arizona, maybe early February. But from the hospital the first day, Marv canceled some repair work for my Beetle that was scheduled for this morning, just in case he wouldn't be available to handle it.

I faced four problems at home in the few days Marv was gone: our front lights on the garage overhang did not go on after dark, even though we just had a new sensor put in; I couldn't get the universal remote for our TV to work; I didn't know how Marv got our neighbor's mail and paper into her garage; and I ran out of milk. All these little things Marv handles. I even forgot to take in the mail on the first day. Just like that I was reminded, as if I needed reminding, of how much Marv does around here and how frustrating it is to have to deal with these problems by myself.

Plus, with my own burning pain in my ribs and long-term, intermittent fatigue from fibromyalgia, Kath has two old people to deal with.

So today I will couch it and read. Marv is busy at the computer.

CHAPTER THREE

In Retrospect

When our time together seemed so uncertain, I often thought about how Marv and I met and how two unlikely people had managed to stay together for so long. Marv would joke and tell others, "It's day by day with Lois." I would joke back and say, "It's not been easy hanging out with him."

I was seventeen when I met Marv on the steps of the administration building of Calvin College—the old campus on Franklin Street. We were both freshmen on a break from taking placement tests.

Because my dad was a minister, we had moved every few years as I was growing up as he accepted calls from other churches or his internal call to become a chaplain during WWII. I was born while he was pastoring a church in Peoria, Iowa. When I was one, he entered the army to be a chaplain. He was stationed on a ship. When it would be coming into harbor, it would be in New York City, so my mother, along with my four older siblings and me, moved to Paterson, New Jersey. An older sister once told me that when my dad came home during that time, the first person he wanted to see was "the baby"—me.

After he was discharged from the army in 1945, we moved to West Sayville, Long Island, New York. We lived in a large, two-story, white parsonage a few blocks from the Atlantic Ocean, where I took my first swimming lessons and learned that jellyfish sting. When I was in the third grade, we moved to Lafayette, Indiana; and when I was in the eighth grade, we moved to Cutlerville, a suburb of Grand Rapids, Michigan. My folks moved again when I was living in the dorm of my hospital nursing program in Grand Rapids, so after I finished the three-year program I joked that I got married because I had no place to go.

Now I can see how my multiple moves as a child have helped me adjust to new situations, meet new people, and make new friends. I like having a "best friend" from multiple childhood places: from New York—she's since died; from Lafayette—we're Facebook friends; and from Cutlerville—we still exchange holiday cards. In fact, it was a friend from Lafayette, where I lived until eighth grade, who introduced me, five years later, to Marv at Calvin College.

I ran into that friend that day on the Calvin campus. Delighted to see him, I exclaimed something like, "I didn't know you were coming to Calvin. It's great to see you." He offered to introduce me to a guy he had met while taking the freshmen college placement tests: Marv Roelofs from Prinsburg, Minnesota.

And there was Marv, outside the "ad building." I was immediately drawn to this tall, thin guy (6'2", much taller than my 5'5") with sandy brown hair (much darker than my dishwater blond), who was raised all in one place (a small farm town southwest of Minneapolis). He had flipped the collar up on his khaki raincoat, Elvis style, and was dangling a cigarette from his mouth—the perfect Marlboro Man of the day. When he stared into my eyes, laughing low and gently at my giggly remarks, I was sure he was God-sent. I had indeed prayed the night before that I would find a boyfriend at college. Later that week, when Marv walked me a few blocks to my carpool and invited me to sit with him at a college-sponsored operetta, I could hardly suppress my flutters. When he put his hand on my leg at the performance, I knew I would marry him.

Sometimes, you just know. I'm pretty sure he felt the same way. He always said he fell in love with my legs first, then my slender ankles. We married three years later, in 1962, the day after I graduated from nurses' training. He had a year of college left.

Words from Marv

After graduating from high school, I signed up to attend Calvin College in Grand Rapids, Michigan. It was at Calvin College in 1959 that I met Lois.

When we met on Franklin Street outside of the college administration building, one of the things that attracted her to me was my smoking. She has told me that I reminded her of the "Marlboro Man," because I had on a khaki raincoat with the collar up, and she thought I was dashing.

Apparently she had prayed the day before we met that she'd find a boyfriend in college. Then she saw me outside the administration building the next day and thought I looked like the epitome of a boyfriend. She fell for me because of my cigarette, and I fell for her because of her legs and ankles.

My mother always called Marv "Marvelous Marv." In the early days of our marriage, when we were still trying to figure out who we were, I didn't like her proclamation. But as time went on, I could see how wise she was, and that as opposite as we were, we were a good match.

I liked attending programs and taking classes; Marv didn't, primarily because he didn't like to sit still for long. But, through give and take, Marv and I worked out a complementary relationship, respecting each other's interests during the day and meeting up in the evenings. He never said no to my ideas, however off-the-wall they were. Go back to school for my bachelor's? Sure. Master's? Yes. Doctorate? Of course. He referred to me as his partner, always seeing and treating me as an equal.

Interests aside, from day one I felt a magnetic chemistry with Marv every time we locked eyes. I loved his squeezing hugs; his knowledge of the Bible, history, and current events; and his ever-present optimism. I even loved his strong opinions about justice, especially regarding the health care of children. Sometimes, however, when his eyelids began to flutter with passion, I would warn him to tone it down.

Early on in our parenting years, an article in *Redbook* gave me the idea for us to write out an informal contract listing who would do what. Marv was game. In addition to the usual guy things of caring for the house, yard, and car, he jotted down on his list grocery shopping and making dinner. Who knew? From that day on, he did it all. Plus, in later years, I'd catch him scrubbing floors and doing the washing.

Above all, I loved how he would listen to me, usually for an hour after dinner.

Words from Marv

On the morning in 1966 or '67, I was supposed to leave our apartment in Minneapolis for my final interview in Chicago for the Cook County Juvenile Court. I got up and was ready to go, and I went to say goodbye to Lois.

She was taking her temperature, which had gone up, indicating she might be fertile.

We had been trying to have a child, but we hadn't been successful. When she noticed her temperature had gone up, she told me I had to go to bed with her before I left. [Author's note: It worked!]

After that, I went to Chicago and my interview was successful. So when I went back to Minneapolis, we prepared to move to Chicago.

Later, when we had our two children and our family was starting out, I was going to graduate school and working for the juvenile court, plus I had a part-time job. That was hard on our family, because I was so busy.

Lois was at home with the kids, which was difficult for her. She didn't like being confined with the little ones. She felt the need to get out and do things. We came to an agreement, to help each other out.

I don't do well studying and Lois needed something to do, so she read my books for me and then told me all about them. That helped me. I didn't have to sit for hours and read, but I could still take the tests and write the papers. Still, I had difficulty even sitting through some of my classes because they could be terribly boring.

Lois started to really struggle with being confined at home. She read a book by Betty Friedan, *The Feminine Mystique*, that made her question her role as a housewife. She also read a quote somewhere that "not everyone is happy with the smell of baked bread in the oven."

That had an impact on her because she realized there was nothing wrong with her for not enjoying being a housewife.

So Lois and I had conversations about how to change things up in our life. Something else she read suggested that parents should sit down and identify what tasks needed to be completed and then split them up.

We figured out what our fourteen tasks were, and I took on the responsibilities of cooking, grocery shopping, automobile maintenance, lawn care, and helping with the kids. She agreed to do laundry and a few other things. We also scheduled when we would watch over the kids. I was responsible for them on Tuesdays, Thursdays, and Saturdays. Those were the three days that worked for my schedule. That meant Lois was free to do whatever she wanted on those nights. She didn't have to stay home— she could go out and be free for a while. It all worked for me. I didn't mind helping out, and I liked doing the cooking.

The only problem we encountered initially was when her folks came to town. Her mom would take her to task if I was in the kitchen making dinner for all of us. Lois liked to remind her that was my job, though. It was a real change for her folks and anybody who came over to our house to see me cooking instead of her. We had a joke that she doesn't even know what to look for in a grocery store because I've been doing the grocery shopping and cooking since 1971.

Jon was born in 1967, Kathleen in 1969. As parents, Marv and I supported each other in our parenting, our careers, and our work to gain advanced degrees; he earned a master's degree in social work in 1971, and I earned a bachelor's, master's, and finally a PhD in nursing in 1991. We'd always been a team; I loved his always referring to me as his partner.

He was indeed "marvelous." And I'd tell him so now and then!

CHAPTER FOUR

January 10, 2018

Email

To: Marianna [my friend for more than forty years, a nurse practitioner]

We saw the internist for follow-up yesterday. He said the labs clearly indicate Marv had a heart attack, but they don't know why. He told us to report any further chest pain right away.

Then he showed us a few "headlights" on the CT scan of the aorta [main artery of the body] done on day two of Marv's hospitalization last week, explaining they were lung nodules [growth of abnormal tissue] and that his lungs were full of emphysematous blebs [small sacs of air]. He warned a biopsy could pop a bleb or two and lead to a spontaneous pneumothorax [lung collapse]. Once, when Marv was in his twenties, for no reason other than his being tall, thin, and athletic, his lung collapsed. Being tethered to a chest tube at that time was such a confining experience for him—neither of us needs that again.

On the other hand, none of this is new to us. We had the exact same scenario before his lung surgery in November of 2010, and that turned out to be nothing.

But then we showed the internist a new lump that had just shown up on Marv's right side below his armpit. You know Marv.

He joked, "We would have found it earlier, but Lois has been remiss in giving me back rubs."

The doctor grinned. "I doubt that it's anything, but we better check it out."

Marv told him if anything bad turns up, we are still going away for our trip no matter what.

The doctor said, "I suggest you go ahead and do what you want to do."

Just that fast, pulmonology called this morning to schedule a PET scan for Friday morning, from Marv's waist up. Then he can have lunch, followed by a pulmonary function test, and a visit with a pulmonary consult who will go over outcomes and a potential treatment plan. We'll hear about the lump problem later.

Sobering. But I'm remembering your motto from when you were dealing with cancer: "It's not cancer until someone says it is."

Marv is encouraged that he feels great and runs circles around all of us energy-wise. He quit smoking for the thousandth time yesterday morning. He is trying the gum again, though it has never helped before.

It's a godsend to get an appointment for the results so soon—a motivator to get things done—and it would be great to know the outcome before we leave for Arizona. Kath knows only that we have a follow-up appointment because she asked. Jon knows nothing.

January 12, 2018

Notes

I'm starting a 5x7 notebook to keep track of doctor visits. It fits in my purse. Marv and I are in a waiting room—I am sitting; Marv is pacing—at the Avera Health Prairie Center, a health ministry described in their materials as "rooted in the Gospel." They treat all people, of course, but it's reassuring to know their spiritual beliefs are similar to mine.

As we drove into the large parking lot in front of the hospital, the signage confirming why we were here threw me a bit. We were indeed at a cancer center. But a cross symbol, signaling we were at a Christian hospital, helped my mind slow down.

I'm reading about Avera's mission on materials as I sit: "On any given day, you will find our physicians and staff praying with patients or encouraging them. Our mission gives us room to infuse God's grace into all our interactions."

"God's grace." Theologically, I've been taught that grace means unmerited favors. As I'm sitting here, I get an idea of how I can start to frame our experience. Good things are happening that I don't believe happened simply by chance. For starters, if Marv would not have had the chest pain, we would not have known to bring him in to be checked. Then we got the follow-up internist appointment right away and now this pulmonology one, including the results of the PET scan and pulmonary function tests, on the same day. If we still lived in Chicago, I doubt we could have gotten the coordinated appointments so quickly.

There's a quote here in the reading material written by a nurse: "I'm happy to be able to offer patients support and compassion during what can be a stressful time. I look at it like this: I'm one of God's tools. He is using me to help get patients to the best that they can be."

"One of God's tools." Wow! I feel right at home with this. Comforted. This is the same concept I taught my nursing students at a Christian college and, of course, the same way I was raised as a minister's daughter and have lived my entire life.

Thinking of comfort, I knew I would need to use all my resources—family, friends, and faith—to walk the path of whatever

Marv and I would have to face. As a teen, sometimes I'd rebelled against my parsonage life: having to behave because my dad was not only the minister but the catechism teacher, whose students were my friends and we were all expected to memorize the answers to the Heidelberg Catechism, like it or not. At the time, that all sometimes seemed too much. As I've grown older, I'm grateful to have a firm grounding in my faith.

Words from Marv

> Prayer, for me, has been an ongoing conversation with God. When I pray, I tell God what is going on, and I ask Him to help me deal with whatever I need help with. I thank God for letting me do what I was able to do during the day and for giving me the physical, mental, and emotional strength to complete my tasks. I always pray for the poor and those who are struggling. I pray for all of the nations, that we will all care for the poor. I also pray that our country will have a revival of ethics.

In Retrospect

Ever since my "piano experience" in high school, I've been aware of God's presence in my life. On that night, my folks were at a church meeting, and I was playing hymns in the living room of our two-story, red-brick parsonage across the street. Out of nowhere, I heard a faint call coming from over my right shoulder and, at the same time, felt as though I were being wrapped in a large, warm blanket.

I remember tears. Joy. Relief. The God I'd been hearing about from my minister dad's pulpit, Sunday School, catechism classes, Young People's meetings, Bible reading after every meal, and years of Christian school felt more personal than ever before.

Other things I'd learned started making sense: I am created in God's image. Jesus died for me. My sins are erased. I will live with God forever. My task is simply to believe and have faith. I began to understand that wonderful word "grace" that God surrounds us with—this gift of unearned love and mercy.

Along the way, as these beliefs became a part of me, the trappings of organized religion have felt less important. In the mid-1990s, when I was in my fifties, I discussed this feeling with a pastor. He explained the development of faith according to James Fowler's book, *Stages of Faith: The Psychology of Human Development and the Quest for Meaning*. He said it sounded like I had moved toward the final stage in which a person (in my words) is not confined by denominational beliefs or theological debates but sees the world in larger terms: a world filled with people who have inherent goodness as fellow human beings also created in God's image; a world of people equally worthy of respect, caring, and justice; a world where my primary responsibility is to try to act accordingly. This gives me a guideline for how to live every day.

CHAPTER FIVE

January 14, 2018

Email

To: Kids and Grandkids [our son Jon, his wife Sheri, and their grown children and their significant others; our daughter Kathleen and her husband Michael, who then share with their young children]

Just so we are all on the same page, I'd like to give you an update in writing on Dad/Grandpa. When we saw his internist a few days ago for follow-up, he had the results of Dad's CT scan of his aorta. The aorta was okay, but there were spots on his left lung, so the internist referred us to a pulmonologist.

We saw the pulmonologist Friday afternoon, January 12, after Dad had a PET scan from the waist up and a pulmonary (lung) function test. We'd already provided results of tests taken in 2010 when Dad had his lung surgery.

The results: There are new lesions on the left side of the lung. They could be new, or they could be as much as seven years old, since we have no measurements since 2010. There is also a new lump on his right side outside his rib cage. We discovered this ourselves just last week. There is a lesion in his left mandible (jaw). He had this in 2010 also, and at that time it tested benign.

His pulmonary function test was almost the same as in 2010, and his oxygen saturation test ran in the high 90s. So all is good there, and he feels good.

The pulmonologist suggested we start intervention with the least intrusive approach, which is to biopsy the new lump on the right side. If that is malignant and it shows itself to be metastasis from the lung, then we will know it is lung cancer. If it is benign, we won't know anything about the lung. Then we will discuss if Dad wants a biopsy for his lung.

Dad is high risk for lung cancer due to age and smoking, but also due to growing up on the farm around moldy hay and pesticides. He says he would inhale moldy hay while working with it, and he used to blow out the spray nozzle on the insecticide with his mouth and invariably take some in.

We see the surgeon on January 23 for consult. Possibilities for what's going on are cancer (of course), benign granulomas (areas of inflammation), or a fungus or latent tuberculosis (which his lung lesion was in 2010).

So we are remembering, as my friend Marianna always says, it's not cancer until someone says it is. We still plan to go to Arizona. We trust and know God will help us deal with whatever comes up. It's been nineteen years since Dad's prostate cancer and then the lung scare in 2010, so we've been blessed! And are grateful! Please keep us in your prayers.

January 23, 2018

Notes

Today we saw a surgeon to have him check the lump on Marv's right chest. Unlike with pulmonology, we'd had to be assertive to get this appointment made before our planned departure for Arizona.

Then, when the nurse checked us in, she said we'd have to make another appointment to have the lump removed. Marv said, "That's not going to happen. It has to come out today. We can't wait around. We're leaving town." The nurse said she'd tell the surgeon.

When the surgeon came in—he resembled a college football player—he said he'd heard the news about Marv wanting surgery today. He lifted Marv's most favorite Australian sweater (textured in bright red, green, and black), looked at the lump, and nodded. "We can handle that here today. We'll get the room ready." Looking at me, he said, "You can come along."

So I observed the lumpectomy. After numbing the area and excising the lump, the surgeon laid the small tumor on the sterile, draped stand that held assorted instruments and lined up a centimeter ruler alongside. I took a picture on my phone. The part excised—pinkish yellow, streaked in red, glistening, with an irregular bumpy shape—was about three centimeters long (a little more than an inch) and half that wide.

I was surprised that I was able to watch and not get queasy. Even though I'd observed excisions as a nurse, I had fainted more recently while with Marv during a colonoscopy. When he'd groaned in pain, I was standing by his feet when the horizontal blinds on the window across the room started to undulate. I lurched to a chair just in time. I wasn't about to tell the surgeon, though. My stoicism during the excision now was probably me assuming my clinical mode. It's sometimes easier emotionally to be more nurse than wife.

I marvel at how things work out Marv's way. It was a given that he'd insist on having the biopsy that day. There is no such thing in his mind as waiting. One of his mottoes is, "There's no such thing as 'can't.'" I would have told him it would never work to have the lump removed on the day of an initial appointment. In his mind, though, we are going to start out for Arizona.

PART II

GETTING SUPPORT

CHAPTER SIX

January 30, 2018

Notes

So finally, standing there at the museum in Dodge City, we knew for sure. The news that would change our lives crashed on us in a second, and Marv's declaration that there would be no treatment landed right after.

I couldn't think that fast. *Why is Marv so determined to refuse treatment?* Once, when we'd discussed the side effects of chemo and radiation, he'd said he would never do treatment, but I hadn't questioned his response at the time. It was before his lung cancer scare eight years ago; that tumor had turned out to be benign.

Right there on the porch of the museum, I turned off the phone and burst into tears. The enormity of what lay ahead hit me hard, right between my eyes. My head pounded. Not again! We'd been here before. How would we deal with the challenge this time? How would I hold up? I realized, almost immediately, that I'd have to muster up more strength than ever before.

Swiping the tears away, I started down the porch steps where Marv was waiting for me. I paused long enough to take his photo staring off into the distance at a row of old stores—City Drugstore, General Outfitting, Saratoga Saloon.

Instinctively, I knew that photo would document the beginning of a decisive change in our lives. *What was he thinking?* I didn't ask. After fifty-five years of marriage, I knew Marv would need time to process the news.

"He said it's serious," I whispered. "Aggressive. He wants you to come back."

I held my breath. Whatever I said would not make a difference in Marv's mind, but I had to make sure he'd heard what I'd heard. We had to be operating on the same information.

"He knows how I feel," Marv said, ending the discussion. "Let's see what we can see here." And he walked off to sightsee.

I had to take a break myself. I found him again in the souvenir shop, regaling an old, withered farmer in bib overalls with stories from his boyhood on the farm. *Incredible. How can he compartmentalize?* Moving on to look for a souvenir, I decided I didn't need or want any Gunsmoke bric-a-brac as a remembrance. The photo of Marv at 76 years old, tall and slender, with salted brown hair and round brown glasses, wearing his brown-and-gray textured Australian sweater, black mock turtleneck, and cords, would be enough.

We found a hotel in a little town whose name I have forgotten. Wordlessly, we went looking for a restaurant. We sat at an old, dark wooden booth, the lone customers there. I looked at Marv and spoke. "It's finally happened."

As we locked eyes, an enormous swell of love and sadness threatened to burst my chest open. Even though we'd lived through previous scares, the emptiness and helplessness I felt now did not compare.

"Yes," he said in a hushed voice that did not waver. "And I'm not going to kick myself for smoking. I know why I did it, and I don't expect others to understand."

We always knew, with his smoking history, that getting lung cancer was a possibility. He had started at age 15 to calm his internal motor, and he had attempted to quit dozens of times. Now he'd accepted his prognosis, which again ended any further discussion.

I turned to a more immediate question. "When should we tell the kids?" Jon was 50; Kathleen, 48.

"I'll call them tonight."

Our meal was a disaster—the burritos arrived dry and brittle with no sour cream or sauce, and the dessert, advertised with a cream-cheese filling and strawberries, came with only canned cherries. The meal mirrored our mood. We ate in near silence while my mind sped ahead to what we would have to do next.

Marv called the kids when we got to the hotel. His voice alternated between strong and broken: "This is Dad. . . ."

I don't remember his words, and I didn't hear their responses; we weren't on speaker phone. I knew, though, that the diagnosis would hit them hard. They loved their dad intensely, but they also grew up with a strong father who, in their eyes, could handle everything from bruised bodies after a tumble to bruised egos from a misunderstanding with friends. *What would it be like for them now, with his days numbered, watching him face certain death?*

That night Marv and I started a tradition that lasted throughout his illness: Marv prayed aloud at bedtime, mentioning each one of our children, their spouses, our three older grandchildren and their significant others, and our two younger grandchildren by name, asking God to be with each one of them in their daily lives.

After Marv fell asleep that first night, I lay in the dark doing web searches on "small cell lung cancer (SCLC)" on my iPad. Marv had asked me to look up whatever I wanted—he knew I would anyway—but he didn't need to know any more about it. He knew it was terminal and that was enough.

I read every reputable entry, aware that whatever I learned would not influence his decision. But I could try to give him enough information to make sure he was making an informed decision, if only for my own peace of mind.

As a nurse, I knew that knowledge is power, and that I'd be walking with Marv during all the unknowns ahead. I reasoned the more I could prepare myself, the less likely I would panic and the more likely I'd be able to pull off whatever would be expected of me. Here's what I learned:

I learned that no treatment could promise a cure for this type of cancer; treatment could delay its progression, but it would return.

I learned that since Marv's cancer was already outside of the lung, it was considered "extensive" or Stage IV, and that the five-year survival rate for Stage IV SCLC was as low as 3 percent.

I learned that SCLC accounts for about 10–15 percent of all lung cancers and tends to grow and spread faster than the other kind, known as non-small cell lung cancer (NSCLC).

And, most importantly at that moment, I learned that untreated SCLC had a survival rate of two to four months after diagnosis. That's all I needed to know; what I didn't know was how long the cancer had been there before it showed up on the CT scan five weeks earlier.

Indeed, as the pulmonologist had warned, we might have only a few weeks.

The next morning, I told Marv I'd read the relevant online literature, and it confirmed what the pulmonologist had said: it could be only a few weeks. He took it in, not saying a word. We had no need to discuss it again.

As he'd promised, we continued on our way to Arizona. While he drove, I tried to make sense of why he was so accepting of his fate. Then I remembered a comment he'd made before we left home.

"I've lived a good life," he'd said. "I've been blessed. If this is God's time for me, I'm okay with it." And considering his age, medical history, and the length of our marriage, I knew I'd been blessed too. In that moment, I found a peace that enabled me to honor his wish to say no to the chemo the pulmonologist had said was necessary. I wasn't sure what that commitment would involve—though I knew he would not want me hovering!

What I didn't know was how I would manage without him.

CHAPTER SEVEN

February 12, 2018

Notes

I'm happy to be settled into our rented condo in Scottsdale with Jon and Sheri [our son and his wife]. We've seen a lot of friends and relatives. On Super Bowl Sunday, we happened to be with old friends in Phoenix. The Philadelphia Eagles beat the New England Patriots for their first Super Bowl crown ever, eliciting a lot of yelling and noise and providing temporary distraction from our story. However, at every stop, Marv eventually told the news. After stunned silences, we received much support for his "no treatment" decision. Several had read Atul Gawande's *Being Mortal: Medicine and What Matters in the End* with its emphasis on determining the patient's priorities before diving into treatment explanations. Clearly, Marv's priority is quality over quantity of life. In one respect, I'm relieved because I know he couldn't sit through long hours of chemo. He'd probably say that would be murder for him anyway.

As we drove, I also spent some time taking his dictation of a few goodbye messages to loved ones—a tough job, but we were very businesslike about it. I would sit in the passenger seat of our Subaru Forester scribbling down his words, which I would type up on my iPad later that evening in a hotel.

To his siblings, for example, he said: "My position is I've had a good life. I'm going to enjoy the time I have left, and I'm ready to go home whenever that day arrives. But for now, I'm feeling very good and have lots of energy. I hope to see each of you in the near future and will send additional updates as they become available."

I wondered at his matter-of-factness; but then I too was sitting there taking dictation as though I did this every day. We were in taking-care-of-business mode, something I would realize later to be part of the shock stage of grief; we felt a numbness toward this actually happening to us and robotically moved through the motions of what we thought we had to do.

Yet, of course, part of me was trying to face facts. I wrote to my two close Chicago nursing friends, who were sure to understand the dire diagnosis as I did, to let them know the situation.

"Marv wants quality of life, not quantity," I wrote. "He feels great and has lots of energy, so it's hard to comprehend. Literature says two to four months without treatment and a few months more with treatment. I have read every website on this and have told him he can expect stuff to happen head to toe. It will not be pleasant. You may recall that my nurse sister died of this a few years back, followed a few years later by her husband with the same thing—lung cancer with metastasis to the brain. Since the docs have stressed 'aggressive' to us and that chemo is the only option because it's already out of the lung, I think I can safely assume it's already in the brain.

"Meanwhile we are seeing lots of family and friends this month on this trip. If Marv starts to deteriorate, we will fly home and worry about the car later. He feels fine now. No symptoms. We're meeting one of Marv's brothers (from Michigan) this morning for church, and then we'll go to a friend's home for a Super Bowl party. Our son and wife will join us soon. That was planned way before any of this.

It seems there are way too many coincidences for them to be only that. I feel God is hovering very close by."

I've been clinging to that feeling of God's hovering every day. After the guys went to bed tonight, I talked to Sheri about how I could handle all the emails I'm getting in response to our news. A friend had suggested a Caring Bridge site. I tried, momentarily, to get that started by uploading a photo there. No luck. I couldn't do this simplest of things. But Sheri tried to reassure me by saying, "Mom, you've always been strong . . ." before her voice trailed off.

On the verge of tears, I barely listened. But I warbled on to her long enough that I came to my own conclusion: I already have a blog; I've been writing there for years. I can use it now to communicate what I need to say. As we hugged goodnight, tension that had been building in my shoulders suddenly burst loose, rippled down my arms, and vanished.

About Me on loisroelofs.com

Welcome, readers!

I started this blog in spring 2010 to center around the fall publication of my career memoir, *Caring Lessons: A Nursing Professor's Journey of Faith and Self.* Since June of 2012, my goal has been to blog, from the perspective of a retired nurse, on writing, growing older, and living in Chicago. And, since 2016, about living in Sioux Falls, South Dakota.

I'm a happy mom of two and grandma to five who decided to take writing seriously in 2000, a few weeks after I retired as professor emerita from teaching nursing at Trinity Christian College.

Working nearly forty years, I held positions in eight places, ranging from hospitals to steel mills, and I taught and/or held administrative positions in four schools of nursing: Prairie State

College, Trinity Christian College, Valparaiso University, and St. Xavier University/Chicago.

I earned a diploma in nursing from Blodgett Memorial Hospital School of Nursing, BHS in Nursing Practice from Governors State University, and an MS in Psychiatric Nursing/PhD in Nursing Science from the University of Illinois at Chicago. And, since I love learning and nurses are known to be lifelong learners, I completed the four-year University of Chicago Basic Program of Liberal Education for Adults in June of 2013.

Until June of 2016, I lived in a Chicago high-rise with my husband; then we moved to Sioux Falls to be nearer to our daughter and family.

Thanks for stopping in! Come again.

February 13, 2018

Blog Post

Two weeks ago, my husband was diagnosed with lung cancer. He's made it clear that while he is thankful for the life God has given him, he will not be seeking treatment.

We both are at peace with his decision, and I have felt enveloped by God's grace these last two weeks as we've united with family and friends in New Mexico and Arizona. Clearly, it's no coincidence we planned this vacation and these visits before we knew about the diagnosis, and God has placed the folks we have visited in our lives exactly when we needed them.

I will be including this experience in the normal flow of my blog at loisroelofs.com. You are welcome to continue following my blog, or to subscribe to it, or to drop in now and then for updates.

In Retrospect

My blog had been a place for my thoughts and self-discoveries for years. Now it would be a space for me to process what was happening.

Back in 2010, when I was preparing to publish my first book (as mentioned above, *Caring Lessons: A Nursing Professor's Journey of Faith and Self*), a writing teacher recommended that I start a blog to promote the book and build a platform. I published my first post on March 27, 2010, and the book launched that October.

For the first few years, my blog centered around my book and its related issues. After that, until Marv's diagnosis in January of 2018, I'd describe my blog as eclectic. I wrote as the spirit moved me, jumping from posts about writing memoir, to nursing, to aging, to birthday thoughts, to a series of ten posts on our move from Chicago to Sioux Falls in 2016.

When Marv was diagnosed, understandably, that became my focus. I started a series of posts titled "Grace Notes" with subtitles. I'll share some of these posts in the coming pages. Here's a few of the responses I got as the months went by:

- "Your Grace Notes document a journey of courage and love."
- "What a courageous road you are traveling."
- "Praying for you and thankful you are willing to share this journey."
- "The pair of you are such an invaluable inspiration to me."
- "I am awed by your strength and courage right to the end."
- "Thank you for keeping this eloquent journal. As a profound testament to Marv and the power of love and faith, it will

help countless others going through similar end-of-life issues."

- "We admire the proactive use of this time with family and friends."

It was helpful and comforting to receive so much support early on from blog readers for Marv's decision for no treatment. My readership for the blog more than doubled during the months of Marv's illness and quintupled the norm during his final month, conveying to me that others around the world were not only interested but may be living with similar situations. I was grateful that sharing our story could help them in some small way.

CHAPTER EIGHT

February 13, 2018

Notes

I continue to worry that it has already been nearly seven weeks since Marv's cancer was first seen on the CT scan. How long had it been there prior to then? And, most chillingly, the doctor's words that Marv might only have a few weeks haunt me. The literature said two to four months, but now it feels like death could occur at any moment. Not encouraging. Not at all. All I can do is pray.

I awoke this morning with a start to find Marv sitting on the edge of the bed next to me. I glanced at the clock: 7:00 a.m. My first impulse was to be angry—it was too early! The day before, he'd been up frying eggs for the four of us and had awakened us for breakfast. I'd told him never to call us that early on vacation. *Why was he waking me up now?*

I opened my eyes wide and glared at him. But something was wrong. His face looked haggard, as though he hadn't slept. "It's time to go home," he said with a heavy voice.

It was two weeks into our month-long trip. Bolting up on my elbow, I asked, "Why? What happened?"

He said he'd awakened at two to a drenched bed. He'd never had night sweats before. He also told me he felt a new pressure behind his eyes and a full feeling in his abdomen. I slid my hand under his T-shirt, and his stomach was harder and more distended than usual.

I sat upright. "Let's tell the kids."

We padded across the kitchen of the small condo we'd rented, and I tapped on Jon and Sheri's door. Soon, we were embracing in a four-way hug next to the kitchen bar, sobbing.

We quickly decided that Marv and I would fly home and that Jon would arrange to have our car returned. By eight o'clock, I was able to get flights on United through Priceline for $54 apiece. I guessed the tickets were cheap because no normal person would want to leave the 70s weather in Phoenix for the 30s in Sioux Falls. We threw things into our suitcases, and Jon and Sheri drove us to Sky Harbor with time to spare for our 1:35 p.m. flight.

A Memory from Jon

When Dad gave us the details of his cancer prognosis in Arizona, I remember his trembling. The trip was not the same after that. We all know we're going to die sometime, but no one knows when. Life can usually be lived thinking really nothing of it. However, once you are told you have a cancer that is growing within you and, without treatment, you will most likely die within six months, I guess you look at life differently.

Dad had his reasons for not accepting treatment. He'd had cancer scares before. About twenty years earlier, he had fought prostate cancer by having nerve-sparing surgery. However, at the last minute, the machine for checking the nerves was in the wrong operating room, and it could not be used. The nerves were not spared, and he lost his continence until he had a faucet-like device inserted many years later. He wore a pad, had many accidents, and just dealt with it. Once, I noticed how, when he would go out and smoke near the trash can, he would replace his pad and just go on with his smoke. I asked him how he handled that and other changes; he said, "What can you do? You just deal with it and go on." Very pragmatic.

February 14, 2018

Email

To: Marianna

We are home. So thankful. Marv was okay on our trip. I'm glad I have you to write nurse-type stuff to! I'm missing my nurse sister Kay. If she were alive, we'd be on the phone a lot. So here goes: Marv's main discomfort is a hard, distended abdomen. GI [gastrointestinal] system is working okay, though. No jaundice in sclera [the whites of the eyes], so I'm thinking his liver is okay. It does feel enlarged as there's a hard area under his right rib cage that's not on his left. His longtime mucous problem in his throat is thicker, and he must struggle to get it out. We both are wondering how this will progress.

We see his internist at nine tomorrow. Our pastor is coming tomorrow afternoon. Marv made these appointments on our layover in Denver. Kath wants to be with us on visits. She is distraught.

Just waking up. So exhausted last night.

Email

To: My Sisters

Marv's out grocery shopping, getting something for Valentine's. The grandkids are coming over after school. Madison [age 8] is wondering if Grandpa is going to lose his hair. Jake [age 6] is oblivious. Don't know exactly what Kathleen has told them.

We're working in our study today. Most of the morning, we sat at our adjacent desks while Marv handed me, one by one, files from his two two-drawer file cabinets, saying, "You'll need this." I made room in my adjacent file cabinet, noting a few file names: cars, taxes, banks, credit cards, insurances. At one point, we both burst into tears. Not for long, but it got the top off during a frantic, tight hug. The worst thing is not knowing how this will progress. Still would like to make some short flying trips.

We got a nice prayer via email from our pastor at Fourth Presbyterian in Chicago and so many nice notes on Facebook and the blog. Too much to take in.

CHAPTER NINE

February 15, 2018

Blog Post

We are home from our trip. Only a few hours after I wrote my post on the thirteenth filled with optimism about our travels, Marv let me know it was time to go home. The word "journey" came to mind; we had to journey home and begin the next part of our journey of living with cancer.

While I made our flight arrangements, I decided I hate all the words associated with cancer—like journey. I don't like that word. Or some of its synonyms: trip, passage, migration. The idea of crossing from here to there. As a nurse, I know living with cancer is not a party, but to make it a journey strikes me as an arduous undertaking filled with negative connotations.

But that's not been true for us so far. This stretch of our lives has had the feel of an adventure. At every turn, we are discovering new things about ourselves, our family and friends, and the world around us, especially all things related to illness. It's a time of learning and feeling unlike almost any other. I say *almost* because Marv has faced cancer before. Each time the diagnosis turned out to be benign or to not need further treatment.

While on our layover in Denver, we ate dinner (Marv had a beef sandwich with fries, and I had a mango chicken salad). Afterwards, I shimmied my spiral notebook out of my stuffed backpack and took notes as Marv dictated things I must do to care for our twin home, the few bushes in the yard, and our two cars after he's gone. We are becoming more aware that we must make productive use of our time.

When our daughter settled us in at home that night, I saw evidence of a recent cleaning spree. We had a sparkling clean refrigerator—items so orderly they appeared alphabetized, with a new light bulb to highlight the lineup—unfamiliar vacuum lines in the living room that I found out were made by our son-in-law, and more. I thought, *I could get used to this.*

And now our son and daughter-in-law, still in Arizona, are arranging to ship our Forester home. After, of course, they'd made a trip to a car wash to clean out the debris of our being on the road the previous two weeks, including the box of aging snacks Marv was keeping behind the driver's seat.

We've received many expressions of caring. I feel like I'm meandering in slow motion in the middle of a parade of God's grace, interspersed with sharing tears of thankfulness with Marv for the life we've had together.

So I'm experiencing this period not as a journey, but as an *adventure*, which has a more positive connotation to me. Of course, we have medical appointments and we know we have hard times ahead, but we have no timeline for the life Marv has left and we will continue to make plans.

He himself has said, "It's like riding a wave of blessings and being propelled toward shore."

Email

To: My Sisters

Marv saw the internist this morning. The main news in the written reports of the chest images was one spot that was 2 mm three years ago in 2015 is now 17 mm. When and how fast did it grow? The internist urged us to see the oncologist sooner than our appointment on March 2 just to hear what he has to say. Marv said, "No, we will wait." No sooner were we home when the oncology nurse practitioner called to offer an appointment the next Wednesday—spooky. Don't know if the internist gave them a heads-up or if it's another God thing. I'm starting to take these providential events for granted. Kath went along to this appointment and will go next week too.

Pastor David from our Westminster Presbyterian Church was here for an hour and a half today. Such a nice guy. Marv also got a sensitive prayer in writing from our pastor at Fourth Presbyterian in Chicago.

Marv is busy at the computer. He made several thousand dollars yesterday selling a stock he purchased recently. He reminds me it's only paper. But he has fun. It's his hobby.

A neighbor and friend are taking us to Minerva's tomorrow night as a thank you for Marv shoveling her driveway. It's nice to have only one restaurant in town that appeals to me right now, so no need to make choices.

I'm very tired. Glad to be on my couch. Marv and I both agree our vacation could not have been better. Just good, with all our lovely encounters. Marv uses the term "beautiful."

So nothing is different here—the internist said if any doctor gives us a time projection, don't listen. With all the possibilities that can go wrong, no one can predict. One day, one year. Tumor growth will determine future symptoms.

We tentatively plan to fly to Florida, since we didn't go there this trip, sometime after Jake's birthday party on March 3. We have four stops planned, along with enjoying the sun.

February 17, 2018

Notes

We had a nice dinner with our neighbors last night at Minerva's downtown. It's a classy place with wooden paneling that reminds me of Gibson's Steak House in Chicago where we used to go for anniversaries and birthdays. I had creamy fish crepes with a side of moist stick-together risotto and the best tiramisu I've ever had.

I always remember that the first time I had tiramisu was after a University of Chicago appointment with Marv for his prostate cancer in 1999. On the way home, I'd wanted to stop at an Italian place on Western Avenue around 103rd Street where I'd been once with friends. I ordered tiramisu that day with Marv, and ever since I've associated it with him having cancer. This isn't necessarily sad—more a poignant point in time when we felt very close to each other.

Today, Marv worked on paperwork all day. He's prepaid stuff for the year. Sobering.

I suggested an outing to the lighting store. We've wanted to replace kitchen and bathroom fixtures. He went, trolled around the store, but then found me and said, "You pick out what you want. I'm not into it," and asked to go home. Kath is heartsick to see him like this. When we got home, I took photos and measurements to send to the lighting gal. She will make up a presentation with illustrations showing us the possibilities.

At night, we vegged and watched the Winter Olympics. They're in South Korea this year. I'm glad they're on. We've always enjoyed watching the competitions and can use the distraction now.

February 19, 2018

Blog Post

Our kids, ages 50 and 48, want to know Marv's stories. I guess it's good they brought it up since his time is now limited to tell them. This strikes me as tremendously ironic because I've been a huge proponent on this blog of documenting your stories. I've warned, more than once, that if you don't write your words down, your words will die with you.

Why didn't I think of documenting some of Marv's stories along the way? I wrote some down so I have a tiny collection, but he's never wanted to be a part of my blog. I've asked him a time or two to write some things and I have hard copies somewhere, but that's it. I have file drawers full of written stories by me, from writing prompts to personal essays, even a novel, but little directly about him.

When we received the news of Marv's diagnosis of "very aggressive" small cell lung cancer three weeks ago, it dawned on me there was still time for me to write some stories. I got out my notebook in the car and asked Marv what life experiences he'd like to tell me so I could form them into stories. But after I had Marv's list, the thought of dealing with the writing was overwhelming, and I pocketed the idea.

Then, while we were in Arizona with our son and daughter-in-law from Washington, our son brought it up. He wanted to know his dad's stories. What stuck out from Marv's childhood on the farm? Outhouses, teams of horses, the party line phone on the wall? And what prompted him to start his business of helping children in special education gain access to needed health care services? And how many children has that affected? And why did he have this lifelong passion for children at all?

Our son forwarded more questions he found online. How could I get Marv's stories written? My mind went blank. Too much was coming at me at once. I soon told our daughter about our son's request. Oh yes, she'd like Dad's stories too.

I thought back to when I did my dissertation for my doctorate. I'd tape-recorded more than a thousand pages of interview data and hired a transcriptionist to type it up. So I thought now, *That's what I could do. Buy an updated recorder, ask Marv to talk, find a transcriptionist.*

I felt better. But my daughter got right back to me. Her husband had two contacts—one a videographer who could film Marv as he told stories, and another who could interview him at length and formulate a legacy book out of his stories. We decided on a book as more lasting, and our son-in-law set it up.

We will spend nine hours in three sittings next week for Marv to be interviewed. The writer then collates the interviews into one cohesive story, adds the pictures we give them, and gives us twenty-five copies of the final book.

Marv is game because he wants his farm stories passed on. This will save me from needing to write his stories. Now it's a big thing I don't have to do.

I'm feeling like a broken record about God's grace, but again, what are the odds of all this coming to fruition with no effort from me?

February 21, 2018

Email

To: All Family [kids, grandkids, my sisters, Marv's siblings]

I woke up sick—bad cough and worn out. I called for an appointment. They had an opening in twenty-seven minutes, but I was still in my bathrobe. I still made it! Something is brewing in my chest. I got some cough medication so I can sleep. I'll start an antibiotic if not better in three days.

While I've had to remember to take care of myself through all this, as usual, Marv makes it easy. I have no outside responsibilities. I can rest when I want to. Over the years, Marv has always picked up any slack if I didn't feel well. He has never made demands on me. Even now, through all this, he continues to make dinner—you know he never has wanted me in "his" kitchen! He likes to tell guests that the few times he let me in the kitchen, I'd set off the smoke alarm. (I only remember that happening once!)

This afternoon, Marv and I saw the oncologist. I had to get a picture of Marv as they discussed the options. He was somber, looking down at the doctor's desk, drumming his fingers, and wearing his sweater again with the blend of multi-textured brown and gray colors that complemented his graying brown hair. A cross on the wall overlooked us as we talked and provided me with a sense of peace.

The plans are all set. No chemo. We've been told that at most, chemo would extend life only a few months, and the cancer would return. So there is no good outcome either way—pain from the cancer or pain/discomfort from chemo, with no cure. The cancer is in the bloodstream, so it's traveling. We'll know how it's progressing by what symptoms occur.

A social worker is setting up a visit from the hospice team to plan for when we need them. They will connect me with a mentor and support group when I want them.

We are very happy with all our young doctors. I truly feel blessed to be here in Sioux Falls right now. Health care is convenient and supportive. The doctor I saw this morning was new to me, and he was immediately sensitive to my wish/need to stay healthy, for Marv. Another God thing.

And good news—after lots of phone work and rigmarole, Jon and Sheri are getting our car back to us by Sunday. At first Marv didn't care about having it, but then he said he wants to make a few more trips to Menards!

We have several appointments for next week and Jacob's seventh birthday bouncy party on Saturday, and we hope to fly to Florida on Sunday to complete our trip. On Facebook, there's a posting where you can hear Jacob singing to himself. So sweet! Grandpa signed his last card to Jacob, which included advice for life. Marv reminded him, "There's no such word as 'can't.'"

The oncologist said that typically, small cell lung cancer patients live weeks to months, but he has no way of knowing—there are always outliers—so Marv should do what he wants to and can. The first we knew of the nodule was the first week of January, so he's lasted almost two months for sure. We are thankful for this time. Grandpa feels good.

We feel your hugs and prayers. Forward this as you wish.

February 23, 2018

Email

To: Gals [my sisters, daughters, adult granddaughters]

We were happy to have Marv's nephew and his wife stop in on their way to volunteer in Rehoboth, New Mexico. Marv shoveled the walk for them, and the plow showed up as they arrived so they could pull into the empty spot in our garage. We shed tears together. Kath stopped over. They were happy to see Kath too.

Marv and I finished up the interview process for his legacy book. We are both wiped but thankful Marv had the opportunity to talk about his life. And it was nice to do the work with fellow Christians. They opened our sessions with prayer and invited us to feel God's presence in the room. Powerful.

My cough is horrendous. Will try water and vaporizer one more day, then have an antibiotic prescription to fill if no more improvement.

Everything is in place for final appointments next week: Taxes on Monday morning. Hospice Monday afternoon. My meeting with two other Chicago transplants to plan OLLI [Osher Life Learning Institute] class later on Monday. My new writing group exploration on Tuesday. Estate review on Thursday. Jacob's party on Saturday.

We'll see about any more traveling. The hospice nurse today led me to believe our time is very limited. Kath will be here for that appointment on Monday.

Sheri—something for you and Jon to consider—if we travel and if Dad dies while we are in Florida or wherever, our funeral home will arrange cremation at that location. Just want you to be aware of the possibility ahead of time that I would not have the body flown back since we are not planning embalmment. We would plan a memorial service a few weeks later on a Saturday early afternoon to make it convenient for folks who work and want to come.

Enough heavy duty for today. We are watching *Wheel of Fortune* and trying to act normal. We'll be going to bed early!

February 24, 2018

Farewell Prayer

At 9:30 this morning, Marv came in from sitting outside. He said, "Get your notebook. I want you to write an email to all our family and friends." After settling down on the couch near him in his recliner, I waited, pen in hand. At times like these, I wished I knew shorthand. But I was able to keep up with chicken scratches because Marv talked slowly, pensively, as if he were carefully formulating the words as he went along. This message went out to about two hundred people.

From: Marv
Dear family and friends,

Hi. It's been an emotional time since receiving the most recent diagnosis of lung cancer, and it's an event that is having daily ups and downs. I'm not so sure what is happening, but I want to share with you something that transpired this morning.

About four o'clock this morning I got up, and, as I usually do, I went to the side door of our garage to gaze outside to welcome the new day. The view of our front yard was awe-inspiring. It was total peace, whiteness covering everything, quiet, not even a breeze blowing. And, in the tree, there's a bird's nest with a nice pile of snow on it. It's a nest that's been open for rent, waiting for birds to come this spring, which is now just around the corner. As I looked at it, I had peace viewing the scene, but also I was very happy to know that soon there'll be new life in the nest, and a new season will begin.

My life has been one of fullness of many blessings, and I'm ready to go, but I also feel pain about leaving. I've approached this whole thing as a situation in which I'm "up to bat." I've had cancer; this is my fourth experience with it. I see myself standing at the plate. I've had three strikes already, but they've been foul balls, so I'm still up to bat. And now I have this new cancer of the lungs; it's been there, but now it's awake. I'm not sure when the final pitch will come, and whether it will be a foul ball or a strike. I suspect it will be a strike, and I'll be out.

My daughter says I have nine lives. Well, not quite, but I've had a number of them, and so I'm going forward with the idea that I've finished. It's been a good life. I know that God will walk with me through to the end, and I can finally go home. I leave with joy and sadness at the same time. I thank you all for your thoughts, prayers, and considerations, and I hope every one of you, too, may have similar blessings as you journey through your lives.

So again, this is just to say thanks. I'm glad I got to know you a bit. Or, you may have touched base with me a bit, and I hope it was positive.

So long, shalom.
Marv

After I typed up the message, I read it to Marv. He asked that I read it at his Celebration of Life service and at his sixtieth high school reunion in 2019 in Prinsburg, Minnesota. I promised I would. He added that "watching the nest" reminded him of a quote from John Milton, another one of his favorite authors in college. He asked me to look it up:

> Gratitude bestows reverence, allowing us to encounter everyday epiphanies, those transcendent moments of awe that change forever how we experience life and the world.

He never stopped surprising me.

In Retrospect

I still marvel at Marv's resolve and his fortitude facing this terminal cancer. Where did he find it? I think of his upbringing on the farm. Marv's Pa and Ma worked the land; they raised cattle, pigs, and chickens; they nurtured nine children. I met them for the first time at their Minnesota farm when we were dating. I remember the strong, tanned arms of Marv's dad, cradling me on the open-air tractor seat, on a bumpy jaunt through the fields. I remember Marv's mother clambering down a steep ladder to a dirt-floored cellar, hunching over a wringer washing machine, and scaling back up the steps with a basket of heavy wet clothes to hang on the line. I never heard them complain about their work. Marv either.

As for me, what helped me help Marv? My upbringing, though in more urban settings, was one of no complaining and of fulfilling obligations. My dad, as a minister, was on call all day, every day. He filled his time with reading, teaching, preaching, and visiting parishioners. My mother taught in grade schools, directed a choir, led women's groups, and entertained endless dinner guests. As the youngest of the five, I learned how to live life in a busy, competent, and organized household.

So I see now that putting one foot in front of the other, doing what had to be done, was the way both Marv and I had learned how to live, and Marv would live that way to the very end.

Blog Post

Marv purged the pantry today. He's been our grocery shopper and dinner maker for nearly fifty of our fifty-five years. I think he doesn't want me to find outdated cans when I take over his role.

This week we are planning for my future. Marv is meticulously going through the motions of teaching me what else I need to know to carry on. He's tutored me on taxes, giving me two spreadsheet pages of what I need to collect, and I took three pages of notes. He's given me the names of the people at the auto dealer, should I run into problems. He's requested referrals from our daughter and son-in-law for a plumber, an electrician, a tax accountant, and an estate lawyer. He wants to see if he can get a new hot-water heater before he goes because "ours is leaking some, and I don't want you to have to deal with that." He's cleaning out his desk drawers, shredding papers I will never need, and transferring the files I will need from his desk to mine.

I went through the motions of taking all the notes, not fully feeling the significance that all of this would soon be my responsibility. I guess I won't know if I can handle it all until I have to do it. Marv has been my support as long as we've been together; I've had the luxury of not having to think about many things that now I'm having to face. Friends have frequently told me how lucky I am, so I know we've had an unusual marriage.

But mostly, I don't want to spend time worrying about those things. I want to live as normally as possible in the time we still have together. This week was full, including the nine hours where we met for Marv's interviews to get his story down in his own words— to dig into his past and relive through passion and tears how he came to be the man he is today. He sat on a straight metal chair, by his request, and I sat nearby on a soft couch, watching. Even with breaks and snacks, the sessions were intense. And exhilarating. Worn out, we had no words driving home on the snow-packed roads of February.

We had our formal "options" appointment with the oncologist. Entering the waiting room, I spotted a Monet waterlily print, a favorite. I bought one when we converted a sunroom to a family room in 1999, when Marv's first cancer was diagnosed. An omen?

Our daughter met us there. When the oncologist came into the exam room, he introduced himself and then asked how we were related to Marv. I'd been to the doctor that morning for a severe cough, so I was wearing one of those pleated aqua masks that showed only my eyes and windblown hair. I mumbled, "I'm his wife." Without pause, our daughter said, "I'm his girlfriend." Marv and all of us laughed. I said, "I share." More laughter. And so that was our introduction to the oncologist.

I took a photo of the slice of PET scan on the computer screen, memorizing the location of the offending stark white areas whose errant travels will take Marv's life. Afterward, we had lunch with our daughter at the cancer center, only I couldn't eat. A smoothie sufficed. This was my fourth trip since 1999 to an oncologist with Marv, so there was no shock value anymore. But it was still heavy. Marv looked and acted the same, but he was going to die. It made little sense. If it weren't for those white areas on the screen, I'd think this was all a very bad dream. Instead, the presence of the disease became a persistent intruder in my mind.

Our daughter dropped in one day after school with our grandson (7) and our granddaughter (8). She had talked with them about things they might want to ask Grandpa. They knew he had cancer and was going to die, and as we'd always taught them, they believed he'd be with Jesus.

Marv sat at the kitchen table and invited the kids over to check out the lump on the right side of his chest. He lifted his T-shirt so they could see and touch it while he explained that this was evidence of his cancer. They reached out hesitantly, their expressions instantly sober. After answering a few questions like, "Does it hurt?" Marv told them they could go play while we adults talked.

Our grandson whirled into the living room munching on his favorite snack from Grandpa—beef jerky—and sang loudly with a big smile on his face, "Grandma's going to be a widow!" His sister followed up, "Grandma's going to live in one of those places where they take care of old people." They proceeded to the playroom singing what our grandson calls "a holy song"—one they must sing quietly, with reverence.

My daughter and I looked at each other as if "Where did those ideas come from?" and had to chuckle. The innocence. The trust that God will care for us no matter the circumstances.

In our in-between moments, Marv and I hug, cry, joke, and watch for changes. He tells me to start looking around for a guy who can cook. This morning we took what he termed his "last" trip to his favorite store, Menards. He stocked up on oatmeal, peanut butter, tuna fish, and chocolates to donate to the needy basket at church. He always includes chocolates "because people deserve to have more than just the staples." It was snowing heavily, and as I waited in the entry for him to bring my Beetle around to pick me up (his SUV hasn't arrived yet from Phoenix), I took in the moment of his rounding the bend and smiled in gratitude. Soon, I will have to get the car myself. I've been very spoiled.

Notes

I cried as I read the above to him, my 500th blog post. Who could have predicted this is how I'd celebrate that accomplishment? Without Marv's support, I could not have taken up writing after my retirement in the year 2000 from teaching nursing.

We are now sitting kitty-corner from one another in our living room—he in his narrow-seated brown leather recliner, me on my beige ribbed-velour couch. When I finished reading, he murmured in answer to many of my questions: "You'll do fine."

I remember words I read this morning in a write-up on the death of Billy Graham: "Remember you never go home alone; Christ is always with you."

CHAPTER TEN

In Retrospect

I have no problem admitting that Marv always did much more around the house than I did. And amazingly, we stuck to the contract we'd written up early in our marriage, renegotiating it every year on our anniversary but never changing because we agreed it worked for us. I did help him a bit with his finance stuff by setting up automatic payments online for our bills, but those are one-time tasks. And I was always our "social secretary," but Marv was not into social gatherings. He thought chitchatting a waste of time; besides, he couldn't just sit somewhere for long without a purpose. He always supported me doing things with my friends, though—movies, plays, lunches, classes, long weekends away with my friend Marianna, and whatever else I dreamed up.

I also kept track of things like Christmas presents, but we didn't make a big deal of them. The few we got for the kids and grandkids I'd buy alone, or he'd occasionally go with me. But he got claustrophobic in stores, so he hated shopping except at his favorite one—Menards. And I planned our trips. He wouldn't have had the patience to deal with the minutiae of all that paperwork. He'd plan the routes first and then turn over to me making the hotel reservations and the arrangements of who/what we'd be seeing and when.

Our system of each contributing what we did most easily or best worked well over the years. Of course I would say that, given

I always had the time and freedom to do whatever I wanted. Now that I knew that soon I'd have to handle all the house, yard, car, and financial stuff, I'd tell my friends, "I didn't sign up for this. It wasn't in my vows."

There's a saying that every successful man has a wife at home taking care of things. Well, I'm that man! I had no idea about all the things Marv quietly and efficiently took care of. And ever since the day of Marv's diagnosis, the question of whether I'd be able to handle it all lurked in the back of my mind. One thing I knew for sure: my day-to-day life would become drastically different.

February 25, 2018

Email

To: Gals

Kath and grandkids joined us for church this morning. Michael is out of town.

Two unreal God things: First, I was sick, so I got up and told Marv I wasn't going to church. Cough. Fatigue. Aches. Then I thought I might be able to rev it up if I ate something. After Raisin Bran, I revived enough to go.

But after one part of the service where we stood for several things, I sat down and wanted to lie down and not get up. I was wiped. Then the second thing happened.

Our cantor, Bailey, a young gal who sings our "Oh Lord hear my prayer" refrain every Sunday, sang a solo:

When peace like a river attendeth my way,
When sorrows like sea billows roll;
Whatever my lot, Thou has taught me to say,
It is well, it is well with my soul.

The words sunk into me, and I shook with repressed tears. We sang that at the folks' and [sister] Kay's funerals for sure. I knew right away I needed Bailey to sing that at Marv's memorial.

And I knew why I'd been led to go to church that morning.

After the service, I went to the front to tell her about my "God things" of the morning. I told her Marv's situation and asked, if she were available, whether she would be willing to sing that song for Marv's memorial. She teared up and said, "I will make that happen."

An unreal morning.

Kath picked up Papa Murphy's pizzas and came for lunch. Then Marv napped for an hour, and me, for three. I woke up with a temperature. I'm on antibiotics since yesterday and forcing myself to drink fluids. With my body aches, I think this cough might become the flu.

Kath will have time alone with Marv tomorrow morning while I have my OLLI Curriculum Committee meeting. Hospice comes at one. Marv is eager to get information on what he can expect.

Marv is still shoveling our driveway when it snows, and he still hopes that we will be able go to Florida next week. He's had a few health scares this week, but they were transient. It keeps us vigilant.

We're watching the Olympics windup tonight. Marv served me dinner on the couch as usual, along with water refills. We joke that I will use his services as long as he is available!

We've received lovely encouraging notes and phone calls. Everything helps.

February 26, 2018

Email

To: Gals

Saw the tax accountant this morning. I forewarned him that my materials next year won't be as organized.

The Avera@Home Hospice admissions nurse came this afternoon. She suggested that Marv has at most weeks, not months, left. She said once a new symptom shows up—like bone pain, slurred speech, or shortness of breath, it would be days. She has arranged for a case manager and social worker to meet with us tomorrow morning to sign the papers to enter hospice. These papers spell out the terms and benefits of this "Medicare/Medicaid/Private Insurance" plan. Kath will be here again for our official signing.

The nurse asked if we've read *Being Mortal*. She said we are a perfect example. She had a student with her and told her ours was a very unusual visit in that we are seeking hospice and that the two of us have accepted the idea of hospice at the same time. Usually acceptance lags behind. We are signing up before a crisis.

Marv also asked about their funding. He told her we had RMD [required minimum distribution IRA] funds that we gave to charity, and he wanted contact info for her organization. She mentioned that she's not ever before had that conversation on an initial visit.

What strikes me as strange is that by tomorrow night, we will have our own Comfort Care box, holding medications for Marv's final days, in the refrigerator. In 2016, I was staying overnight with sister Esther before the Calvin College Faith and Writing Festival when brother-in-law Dave was on hospice, and we had to call the nurse with a question about his breathing at 1:30 a.m. Esther made the call and told the nurse to talk to me, her sister, because I was a nurse. The nurse asked me to ask Esther whether she had a Comfort Care box in the fridge. Esther got it, and the nurse told me what medications to give Dave. That was a Wednesday night. He died on Sunday. And now it's our turn to have a box.

Looking forward to a quiet evening. Feeling a tremendous sense of peace and gratitude that we're able to take care of all loose ends in a timely fashion. God is watching!

Email

To: Chicago Writing Friends [two women from my long-term critique group]

Marv is insisting I go ahead and live my life. I'm thinking of planning to attend the Iowa Summer Writing Festival again and am interested in the first two sessions by Joseph Martin. Thought I'd check if you gals may be interested in going. I would fly from here.

I can't even believe I'm planning like this, but it helps me stay sane in an unreal time. Marv still feels okay, but we understand it may deteriorate quickly. We are having some good times. Thankful.

February 27, 2018

Notes

Our hospice nurse Sara came today with our social worker Kelly. What a great fit. I'd alerted the admission nurse that Marv didn't have a lot of patience, so I asked them to please send someone who could work with him. Ever the advocate, am I! Sara and Kelly are perfect. Marv took to Sara right away; she's blond, fortyish, with a quiet demeanor as she set up her laptop on our counter-height kitchen table. She managed to keep Marv, sitting opposite her, on his chair rather than on the edge as if ready to bolt. They quickly established commonalities—her farm background and interest in special education children. I was a bit worried at first about social worker Kelly because she was much younger, but she read Marv's wariness correctly and immediately started to josh with him.

This first visit, around our kitchen table, was a success. Sara told us of the services hospice will provide: she'll come once a week, and aides can come up to ten hours a week for housekeeping, bathing, and showering. We'll have access to their chaplain and music therapist. Kelly will come every few weeks. Marv's regular doctor will be the attending physician and will sign off on all medications, which are included. Medications will be delivered to our home. If we need it, hospice will provide equipment like a walker, commode, hospital bed, and wheelchair, along with portable oxygen for travel and incontinence supplies.

Our benefit period is ninety days. If we need hospice longer, our case will be reviewed and extended. This is very comforting! Even to think Marv could last longer than three months gives me hope.

Sara also told us short-term acute hospice care is available. She explained it as an intensive care unit for hospice. If Marv has a need for symptom management, like nausea, vomiting, pain, or restlessness, he can be admitted to their hospice house for five days every benefit period.

Sara made sure we understood that we have the right to withdraw from hospice at any time, but if a patient is on hospice care, that implies they are not seeking medical care designed to cure the patient. If Marv does want to see his own doctor or be admitted to a hospital for care, hospice would be suspended. Hospice is intended for end-of-life care only, when further treatment isn't an option or not wanted.

What she said suits Marv fine; he is sure he wants no treatment or further testing.

The best thing for me is that there is a nurse on call twenty-four hours a day. I will have backup! I immediately put the phone numbers on my iPhone.

Sara gave us the information to order a Comfort One bracelet that tells emergency personnel—say we have an accident on our travels—that Marv has a do-not-resuscitate order. Not all states honor this, so I must also carry a copy of his DNR order in my purse. If we travel, I must send Kelly our itinerary. If we run into a health care problem, all I need to do is call in and they will connect us to care where we are located. Another relief to know.

Then Sara did what she said would be her normal activities each week: ask Marv's weight, listen to his heart and lungs, and take his pulse, blood pressure, and oxygen saturation level. Marv smirked at me: "See? My lungs are still good." He always likes to have the last word.

Neither Sara or Kelly hurried; they both listened to every one of our concerns. As I entered these notes in my little notebook, I wanted to shout out to everyone to go on hospice right away when you're ready to stop treatment. I thought of friends who died soon after they went on hospice; one even died as hospice was delivering the hospital bed. I want everyone to know about the backup and support that can give immeasurable relief.

After Sara and Kelly left, Marv grinned at me as if to say, "We made the right decision," refilled his coffee cup, and loped off to his computer in our study, obviously happy the meeting was over and had gone well.

In Retrospect

Our siblings' experiences with dying must have played a part, unconsciously, with how I was handling my caregiver role. Between Marv and me, we had five siblings in recent years who cared for their spouses at home until death. Because none of them lived nearby, I read many emails dealing with a terminal diagnosis, hospice visits, and funeral preparation. These details were fresh in my mind.

In the back of my mind, too, was my experience teaching crisis intervention to my nursing students, a theory that suggests if a person finds successful ways to handle a crisis, they will have a repertoire to draw from during the next crisis. I'd cried for days with Marv's prostate cancer in 1999, and it was months before I felt normal again. I'd written lists and lists of what I would have to know and do. In 2010, with his lung cancer scare, I'd written, while we were going through it, a 50,000-word novel in a month, fictionalizing the experience. By the time this cancer arrived, list-making and writing in times of crisis were old friends and gave me the repertoire I needed.

February 28, 2018

Email

To: Marianna

Marv tentatively negotiated a new car for me yesterday, in which he would trade in his 2017 SUV and my 2000 Beetle, and he told me about it when he got home. My initial reaction? No way! However, I didn't want to hurt his feelings—he even told me it came in my favorite shade of blue. But after a few hours of gut ache, I got up the gumption to say no no no to everything. I'm simply not ready to give up my comfort car or to think about a new one.

I'm proud of myself.

And I ordered a Shabby Chic floral bed quilt just now. When the time comes, I want a feminine look. I will need a new feel in our bedroom for sure. I got our current duvet cover when we moved to downtown Chicago in 2005. It's time.

I'm feeling empowered.

I felt well enough to go to a new writing group last night. I'm the great-grandma of the group. All are thrilled I got us together. We'll meet the last Thursday of the month from five till eight and submit up to ten pages a week before for critique. All have self-published, with an acceptable number of sales to them. All are full of dreams and energy. It will be a new trip for me. There are four of us now; we will look for two more so that if some are absent, we'll still have a decent-sized group.

Marv and I have our final legal appointment this afternoon. Hope to leave Sunday for a farewell tour to Chicago and Grand Rapids. Have oxygen concentrator and Comfort Kit already and the Do Not Resuscitate sign on fridge.

March 2, 2018

Blog Post

We had hospice in and out all week—two nurses, one social worker, one chaplain, two delivery people. We met with an accountant and a lawyer. Both were sensitive to our situation. Both will expedite whatever must be done.

And, my haircut turned out. Yeah, I know. This isn't the most serious thing. But I haven't found the exactly right hairdresser here, and I greatly miss my gal in Chicago. But going in, I said to God, "You are making everything smooth here, so I'm confident this will go well too." And it did. I hope that doesn't sound too flip or sacrilegious, but that's the way this adventure has been going.

My daughter had booked us massages; Marv's was last week, mine this week. The therapist said little until the massage was over. But as I was leaving, she said quietly, "Your husband told me he's at peace and he's ready. May I give you a hug?" After we hugged, she said, "I'll be praying for you. And you know I'm at Avera's Prairie Center almost every day, so when you're there, feel free to look me up."

When I left the fitness center (also affiliated with Avera) where the massage therapist works, the receptionist motioned me over: "I know what you're going through. We are all praying for you here." Every display of concern brings tears.

Adding a few more to the many God sightings this week: Last Sunday, a church we attended nearly twenty years ago had a note in their bulletin about Marv. This week he's received lovely notes with memories of his work there many years ago. And, our car finally arrived from Arizona.

Above all, Marv feels well, and Lord willing, we'll travel next week and make a final hug tour to Michigan and Illinois for him to say goodbye to family and friends. Our son will fly in from Seattle to Chicago and make the trip home with us to Sioux Falls. We will be surrounded by love. And of course, we will be in God's hands.

March 3, 2018

Email

To: Blodgett Memorial Hospital School of Nursing, Class of 1962 (annual class letter)

We've had a good year and a half in Sioux Falls. However, our lives are topsy-turvy right now as Marv was diagnosed about a month ago with small cell lung cancer.

We are both at peace with his decision to opt out of treatment. I've been blogging about God's grace through this latest event in our lives, and I see God's hand as pivotal in guiding us to move here. I'd always said if something happened to Marv, I'd want to live by my daughter, and now here I am.

Over Christmas, we had gone with our daughter and family to Aruba. That is Marv's very favorite place—he loves the ocean. He's never been a pool guy, so it's like that trip was also meant to be. He spent hours every day in the water and loved introducing our grandkids (6 and 8) to the ocean.

Last fall, Marv and I took a Vikings Homeland Ocean Cruise. We'd never been to the Scandinavian countries, so we enjoyed the history and scenery. We had decided that was the last foreign trip we wanted to make, so, except for some US travel, we've completed our bucket list.

This morning we attended our grandson's seventh birthday party at a bouncy house. I got great pictures of Grandpa sliding down a huge inflatable with both our grandson and granddaughter. We are making as many memories as we can. Marv still feels well, so it seems like we are living in a dream.

Notes

At Jacob's bouncy party, Marv wept.

I was standing in the middle of the large bouncy room Kath had reserved for the party, full of big red, blue, and yellow inflatables, watching the kids to ensure they didn't jump on each other, when Michael walked over to me. "Dad's crying."

"Where is he?"

"Over there. In the corner. Behind the treat tables."

I scanned beyond the inflatables and spotted Marv seated in a darkened corner. I rushed over and took the chair beside him. He was openly weeping. I took his hand. Between deep sobs, he said, "This may be the last birthday party I'll attend. I may not see the kids grow up."

My jaw tightened. I swallowed hard. Tears leaked down my cheeks. The enormity of our situation hit again. *What can I say?* I whispered, "I know; I'm sorry." We sat in the darkened corner, hand in hand, until his sobbing stopped.

He regrouped and sauntered over to cheer on the birthday boy Jake, who was trying to jump from the top of one large ball to another to a final landing place. As he repeatedly slid off the first one, he said, "I can't do it."

Marv said, "There's no such word as 'can't.'"

Marv started to cheer. Jake kept trying. Finally, Jake got the hang of it, jumping from ball to ball, splaying himself on each one, grabbing at the wide surface to stabilize himself, then gingerly balancing to stand for the next jump. When he nailed the final landing, the look of pride on his face, accompanied by the boisterous cheering from Grandpa, crushed me with sadness. I got it all on video from the sidelines.

PART III

SAYING FAREWELL

CHAPTER ELEVEN

March 12, 2018

Blog Post

We are now home from our whirlwind six-day, 1,600-mile "last hug" trip.

At the end of February, Marv, still healthy, had asked me to organize a "last hug" tour to family and friends in Grand Rapids, Michigan, and Chicago. I worked up a schedule for the following week, sent it on to the folks he wanted to see, and said I hoped it would work for them.

Along the way, some people asked if we'd heard of *Driving Miss Norma*. We hadn't, so I looked up the Facebook page her children started when their 90-year-old mother was diagnosed with cancer. She'd refused treatment, saying she "wanted to hit the road" and then traveled with her kids the final year of her life.

Marv had wanted to "hit the road" too; he wanted to say farewell and give hugs to several siblings, nieces, nephews, friends, and employees. He drove all but the last 250 miles of the trip. Our son flew into O'Hare on our final day, and after we'd stopped for dinner in St. Charles, Minnesota, he drove the final way home. I was relieved because it was then dark and time for Marv to have a break. It was a good trip.

Yet here's the thing: it's not nice getting a cancer diagnosis. It's not nice wondering what day it will be that Marv will tell me he's noticed a new symptom. It's not nice not knowing when the cancer will kill him. We've been told Marv will be going full tilt, and then he won't. There will not be a slow demise.

Still, we have been given some time. Being able to make this farewell hug tour was a huge gift. We knew of Marv's cancer only because he had chest pain on January 3. Had he not had the chest pain, I would not have taken him to ER. We still would not know he had lung cancer, and we would not know his days were limited. We would not have had the opportunity to become so intentional about our day-to-day lives.

We remain grateful.

Marv would like to take more hug tours—there are more siblings and friends to see—but we will decide that as we go along. Now, we look forward to a visit from our adult grandchildren; they'll be coming in from out-of-state later this week.

In Retrospect

During this time, Marv and I were having multiple talks on where else to go. Marv desperately wanted to fly to Texas to see a sister we'd been planning to see on the way home from Arizona via Florida on the trip that got cut short. I could not see any way that I could handle the possibility that he might get worse on any trip that required flying. The Comfort Kit would fit into my backpack, but no way could I handle the bulky, box-like oxygen concentrator that weighed at least fifteen pounds. The hospice nurse confirmed that air travel would not be recommended at this time.

Still, Marv kept insisting he wanted to go. I had to remind him, gently, we should take it day by day to see how he felt. At last, he must have realized flying would not be possible because he began planning more road trips. The hospice nurse and social worker assured me that if we ran into trouble, we could call them; they would put us in contact with a local hospice.

That was reassuring, but this scene replayed itself in my mind: Marv driving 75 mph on I-90 toward Chicago, suddenly becoming short of breath, jerking us off the highway onto the shoulder. Me flying out of the car, opening the trunk, hauling out the concentrator, hooking him up to oxygen with semitrucks honking and swerving around us. Marv, gulping for breath. Me, modeling short, even breaths and reminding him not to panic. Calling hospice. Waiting for a return call. Watching the desperate look of air hunger in Marv's eyes. Feeling helpless. Baking on the sun-drenched highway in Wisconsin. Marv gasping. . . .

When I told that scenario to Marv, he said, "You worry too much. I would drive until we got to the next city."

There were days I did not appreciate his optimism.

March 19, 2018

Blog Post

I told a friend today that I was ready for a humdrum normal day. Marv is still going strong. Last week he washed both cars one day and mopped our ceramic tile floors on another. Meanwhile, my cough has not gotten better; as of today, I'm on steroids and an inhaler. "Not fair!" I scream. "Marv is the one who is supposed to be sick, and I'm the one who is dragging."

Aside from that, I've told several people lately that God continues to sit firmly on my shoulder. It's so reassuring to have the constant awareness that I'm not traveling this road alone. God is a comforting presence walking with me and caring for me throughout life—I feel it every day.

Last Monday, at morning fellowship with a group of women from my church, my job was to provide the discussion topic. Based on all my what-are-the-odds, God-sighting, providential events in the last few weeks, I asked each person to share hers. I started by sharing two of mine.

First, a person who backed into our car on our February trip to Arizona turned out to be a friend of the owner of our local repair shop here in South Dakota. That person called Marv while we were driving to Michigan and said he was arranging the payment of the repairs with his friend. Really, now—a random person in Arizona knows our repair guy in South Dakota.

Second, during that same trip, Marv had just said to me that my hair looked really bad—that was okay because I agreed with him— so I messaged my former hairdresser in Chicago on Facebook, on a Sunday morning from our car, and asked if she'd have an opening on the day we were going to be there. She answered immediately; she'd heard about Marv from a mutual friend, was going to reach out, gave me a time, and signed off with, "OK, Luv. Giving you a big hug. Can't wait to see you." Really, now—she happened to be on Facebook Messenger at the same time as I was on the morning of her day off and happened to have an opening when she's usually booked weeks ahead? Or, maybe she made an opening for me.

Other instances I didn't share: I discovered the hostess of my new-to-me book club was the predecessor to our hospice chaplain. Really, now. And, after a salesclerk asked me numerous times if I was looking for anything special—and in desperation, I finally answered, "Yes, I am. I'm looking for something to wear to my husband's memorial"—she disclosed that she used to be an oncology nurse, asked about my husband's cancer, and asked to give me a hug.

Really, now.

Then all our adult grandchildren from out-of-state—three, plus their significant others—came for a long weekend. Truly it was another God thing to have all six in the same room at the same time, sharing stories. We hadn't been all together in a long time. We shared laughs and tears and wound up the weekend with prayers of gratitude for each other and our faith.

My last story for now: A few weeks ago, I'd mentioned to a gal at church that Marv's lifelong favorite song was "In the Garden." And yesterday morning, as Marv and I sat in church with our six young-adult grandchildren lined up next to us in the pew, the choir sang:

> I come to the garden alone,
> While the dew is still on the roses,
> And the voice I hear falling on my ear
> The Son of God discloses.
>
> And He walks with me, and He talks with me,
> And He tells me I am His own;
> And the joy we share as we tarry there,
> None other has ever known.
>
> He speaks, and the sound of His voice
> Is so sweet the birds hush their singing,
> And the melody that He gave to me
> Within my heart is ringing.
>
> I'd stay in the garden with Him,
> Though the night around me be falling,
> But He bids me go; through the voice of woe
> His voice to me is calling.

Can you feel the emotion that swept over me? See my tears?

I can only conclude God is faithful, God is kind, and as we learned long ago in catechism, God is omniscient, omnipotent, and omnipresent. And did I mention our pastor's sermon was on *knowing* God—as in *experiencing* God, not simply *knowing about* God?

I wouldn't recommend getting cancer to have the profound experiences we are having, but it's been a huge wake-up call to slow down and listen for God's presence.

March 22, 2018

Blog Post

We are having a break now from our relentless focus on the diagnosis of cancer; we are finished with most of the paperwork and farewell visits.

Last Tuesday, we drove to Marv's hometown in Minnesota, concluding the visit of relatives there with a stop at the cemetery. He wanted to express "see you soon" sentiments to his parents. Then yesterday, he turned 77, most certainly his last birthday. We planned nothing. I baked no cake—Marv has never wanted or liked cake. We had frosted donuts, leftover brownies, and coffee-cake braids from the weekend. Enough already—time to eat lettuce.

Then our daughter showed up after school with our young grandkids, at the same time as our older grandson, with B&G chipwiches for all. (For nonlocals, B&G is the premier caloric provider in Sioux Falls of ice cream concoctions.) My chipwich tasted crunchy, smooth, and chocolaty, all at once. Since Marv did not eat his, I said, "They only last twenty-four hours, so don't be surprised if it disappears from the freezer. Any ice cream aficionado knows it would be a shame to waste something so special." He didn't respond right then, but there would be a moment later when he got back at me.

I'm glad when our humor can play out normally. After being bombarded for several weeks from the medical establishment with the word "aggressive," we are very tired of that word. It's difficult to tell how aggressive this cancer is. Marv has no symptoms; he's always run circles around all of us, and he continues to do so. Often it feels like he and I are talking about someone else as we take care of the nitty-gritty details of impending death.

So with no obvious changes, Marv is wondering if he still has cancer. He tells folks that since being on hospice means he'll get no more tests, we won't be able to see how the cancer is spreading, or not, through his system.

No matter. We are always on the alert for the "change." What will happen first? Bone pain, shortness of breath, confusion? This last is where some humor comes in. We are keeping tabs on who has the most "senior moments." Sometimes it's me, and I claim that's not fair.

I've told Marv that patients often die after a significant event they were looking forward to or after the last child flies home and enters the room. So he's decided to keep on planning things. Cutting down the tall grasses on the berm in our backyard. Hitting the road again—in April to take a southern route to visit more friends and family, in May to attend a sister-in-law's ninetieth birthday party in Michigan, in June to drive back to Michigan to attend a grandniece's wedding. Picking apples and making applesauce once more in the fall.

When I hear him voice these thoughts to others, I add, "As ornery as he's always been, he'd be the one who could pull this off."

Meanwhile, he tells me things like this: "We were down to one stamp, so I went to the post office today and got you stamps."

On getting new kitchen and bathroom lighting we'd planned for this winter, he said, "Just wait until after I'm gone and get something you like. I can't get excited about this now."

We have a loaner car for four days while our SUV is getting repaired, so he issued this warning yesterday: "If you need to return the loaner, don't forget to remove our garage door opener."

On my saving a stamp that came in the mail today: "You are saving well! Pretty soon you'll be saving napkins too." (He never tosses any unused, or slightly used, home or restaurant-issued napkin. A family joke on him.)

When traveling over snow-covered highways: "Those crops are really doing well." I look out at snow-covered fields. I know I'll never get the farm girl in me, but I do know crops don't grow in winter. I look at him, "You goof. There are no crops now." He says, "Made you look, though, didn't I?"

It's good to joke, to provide some levity with the heaviness of not knowing exactly what lies ahead. When our son (as our power of attorney for property) told me not to worry, he'll give me a $10-a-week allowance, I said I'd make sure that I hit Michigan Avenue when we were in Chicago while my credit card still works. And with our daughter as our power of attorney for health care and her former career in long-term care, I'm watching that I don't repeat myself too often or she's threatened that I'll be earning my keep in a place by folding linens. I tell her I'll be running the nurses' station.

Now, looking forward to more travel, this cancer adventure feels like we're always planning a trip. Marv outlines the itineraries; I make the reservations. Planning is a fun time of looking forward to getting away. I liken this joyous planning time to Marv's final trip that he calls "crossing the Jordan." Certainly, it's the happiest-ever kind of trip for him.

But when I think about it too much, it's not at all happy for those of us he'll be leaving behind.

For the time being, we sit here in our living room—me on my couch, he in his recliner, like some old folks, happy to have a boring evening at home. The most excitement here is seeing which one of us can get the most correct answers on *Wheel of Fortune*.

As usual, my voice broke as I read the above to him. "It's emotional," he said, with lips and cheeks quivering. Then he collected himself and chuckled, "You can—I mean, may—have the chipwich."

Words from Marv

Since I believe in using our talents and not being wasteful, I started making applesauce when we moved to Sioux Falls nearly two years ago.

It's become a bit of a joke—here comes Marv with his applesauce. Maybe it's an unusual activity, but it's something I enjoy, and everyone who has received some applesauce has enjoyed it. Even the seniors and the Wednesday night kids at church.

There was one lady who worked at the bank who did our mortgage; she really enjoyed my applesauce. I ran into her recently, and she asked me if I had any more. I hadn't given her any this past year since we didn't have any banking to do with her. She told me she wished she had called me because her kids were asking about my applesauce. I told her I might get around to making some more. After all, I'm not going yet. Maybe I'll stick around long enough to get some apples picked.

Making applesauce sort of represents living life to its fullest.

CHAPTER TWELVE

April 2, 2018

Blog Post

When I was a psychiatric-nursing graduate student in the 1980s, I did a clinical practicum on an oncology unit. As I live through our "waiting game" now, I remember what one of my patients said. He'd been given six months to live and had outlived his six months. He said, "I've said goodbye to everyone, and now I feel like I'm just a bother hanging around."

While we settle into this period of outliving the dire predictions Marv received upon diagnosis, I can say Marv doesn't feel this way. In fact, he's still busy with his usual activities and planning our next trips. Recently, he wrote an Easter note to family and close friends, and—if I pay him a royalty fee—he said I could use excerpts here:

Happy Easter! Your thoughts and prayers have been very effective! The response from so many has been overwhelming for Lois and me. Every day I continue to have lots of energy and remain very busy doing things around the home and in the community. I'm thankful for the extra time I have been given and don't know what the next health event will be or when it will occur. Each day I get up at 5:00 a.m. (don't know why), but I go outside and greet the new day with a "Thanks." . . .

I was warned my life expectancy would be maybe two months. Now, we are entering our fourth month, April, assuming the cancer was there before discovery in January. I've experienced no changes in my health. It has been an emotional time for both Lois and me as we wonder when it will happen.

We traveled to Grand Rapids, Michigan, and Chicago in early March. I visited my company's office in Frankfort, Illinois, and met with staff and retired staff members. One of them, a strong Christian believer, placed her hand on my shoulder with my permission and prayed that God would take this cancer out of me and cast it on the ground. I didn't see anything exit; however, since then I have been feeling very good and energetic. Now, I wonder if the cancer is gone or if I have only been given additional time to transition our finances to Lois? Perhaps God has given me the extra time since finances are not one of Lois's real interests. . . .

It is indeed an unusual time to experience and very emotional. In many ways, it has been very positive for Lois and me—very rich! . . .

With love and thanks to all for your thoughts and prayers,

Sincerely, Marv

Our immediate family has now all been here to visit. Our daughter-in-law flew in last week from the West Coast. She provided us with pleasant relief, after we'd had an iffy day wondering what we should do with our "extra" time. She listened while I babbled on about everything from the floral bed linens I bought because I'm not sure I'll be able to handle sleeping with the same plain linens if Marv dies in our bed, to my making a therapy appointment to set up that support system for when I'm alone.

You can see how my mind travels hither and yon as I engage in anticipatory planning. And grieving.

We had a fun, light moment too. My husband has always been on the move. He readily admits he can't sit for long. That's very convenient for me. When I'm on the couch, I watch to see his body lean forward in his recliner. Then I issue my requests. "While you're up, I'd like my water glass filled / a Frango Mint from the freezer / my reading glasses from the bar. . . ." Except for bathroom trips, I can stay on the couch from dinner time, when he serves me there, until bedtime, after the evening news.

So, when Marv asked our daughter-in-law if she'd like a piece of jewelry holding a bit of his cremains, she and I looked at each other and grimaced. I said, "I'm not sure I want you hanging around my neck." We researched other possibilities. Perhaps a paperweight? We all cracked into laughter when our daughter-in-law said, "We could say we finally got you to sit."

Now we look forward to whatever the next few days or weeks or months will bring, knowing the faith and prayers and support that have carried us this far will continue to do so.

Meanwhile, another hug tour is in the planning.

April 3, 2018

Email

To: My Sisters

I still have my cough and am in a huge fibromyalgia flare. Every part of my body burns. Have cut sweets and most carbs because that has helped before. But nothing can take away the stress of not knowing "when."

I've talked Marv out of driving to Texas to see the one sister he hasn't seen yet. I could not handle 3,000 miles between April 4 and April 15, then fly out on April 16 for the five days in Chicago I'd planned long ago with Marianna. So we will do just Kentucky instead. We leave tomorrow, Wednesday. Arrive in Berea, Kentucky, Friday afternoon (1,000 miles). Dinner and stay over with a nephew of Marv's and his wife. Will be fun to see their life.

April 14, 2018

Blog Post

We spent a week on the road, traveling southeast to Missouri, Kentucky, and Indiana and visiting several nieces, nephews, and friends. Marv drove all two thousand miles. I came home worn out, while Marv still had his usual energy.

I'll always remember the warm conversations and laughter we had with several of our nieces and nephews. Each had lost one or both parents, siblings of Marv or me. I could feel our siblings' presence as I sat with their children. I wanted to tell our siblings how well their children had turned out. I wanted to tell them how respectfully they listened to our cancer story. I wanted to tell them the stories we heard about their grandchildren.

I don't think our siblings' children could appreciate the poignancy of our time together—to hear an inherited chuckle, to catch a familiar mannerism, and to see a physical resemblance felt like rare, fleeting gifts.

No doubt I'm more conscious of death and the loss of loved ones right now. Even though Marv still has no symptoms, we are vigilant each day for something to happen. We were no sooner home than our hospice nurse and social worker came over. Even if we try to live as normally as possible, there is this shadow that hovers.

Marv and I have spent more time together these past few months than ever before. We've never been a joined-at-the-hip couple. We've always respected our separate lives and interests, while meeting up in the evenings.

He had a great way of explaining how a relationship can be both together and apart and still thrive. Once, when he was being fitted for new glasses, the young gal helping us said she was getting married soon. Marv abruptly stopped the fitting: "I have some advice." He held up his hands, flat with fingers spread out, palms facing her, and showed her that only two fingers of each hand (any two fingers— he used his index and middle fingers) can touch those of the other hand at a time. "These are the two fingers showing the connection between you and your new husband. The others are free to connect with whatever supports the growth of you as an individual."

She looked at him with eyes widening by the millisecond. I thought, *She must be thinking this guy is way off base to suggest she not try to rotate her wheel to try to meet all her new husband's needs.*

I looked on with an amused smile. I'd heard his "marriage as a partnership model" many times.

He went on to say, "That's what my wife here and I have lived for over forty-five years. I've been free to start a business, and she's been free to pursue the schooling she wants. She'd never want to be a part of my business, and I'd hate to take classes forever like she does."

So this being together 24/7 is new to us. Marv and I agree it's time for a bit of a break. We've said all the things we've wanted to say. I've learned about all I can absorb about caring for our home and finances. Even on this last trip, Marv explained several spreadsheets of information to me. He has a unique-to-him manner of filling out spreadsheets—some information reads top to bottom, while other information reads left to right. So it's up to me, the student, to follow his train of thought. My pencil is busy drawing lines and arrows, so I can document connections he sees that I don't. And, after being sequestered this weekend in the worst April snowstorm in South Dakota since the mid-1990s, we are more than ready for some separation.

So next week I will spend five days in Chicago with old friends. Our daughter will be "on call" for her dad. But her dad wants no help! He's fine, thank you. He'll be busy in the garage making wooden lockers with slide-out bins and doors with handles for our grandchildren.

Don't bother him. He'll be enjoying his peace and quiet.

Words from Marv

> I like to make things, so I built a ladder that went over our fence so other neighborhood kids could climb over into our backyard. . . . I bought a swing set for the kids and put that up in the backyard. It had a double bar at the top

and a teeter totter. I thought they needed a clubhouse, so I built them one on top of the six-foot-high swing set. It had a ladder leading up to a deck I put on top. The kids tried playing up there before I even had the walls up. I had to keep them off of it until I was finished. When I finished putting it together, they really enjoyed it. They could go to the backyard and swing and slide and sit in their clubhouse. That thing stood there for probably fifteen years, I think.

April 16, 2018

Email

To: My Sisters

Last night Marv gave me another "after I'm gone" talk. I went to the bedroom and cried. He tells me to be thankful we've had this extra time together. It all feels surreal as he's now busy in the garage like normal.

April 23, 2018

Email

To: Marv's Siblings

No real changes for Marv. We are thankful for each day and mindful, as his doctors have said, that things may change quickly at any time.

We are staying put in May. Marv is signed up to give three children's sermons at church. If he is still well in June, we may go to the Grand Rapids area for the wedding of one of my grandnieces. Marv would be able to say his goodbyes again! We feel blessed.

April 25, 2018

Blog Post

"Be open to God's work in your lives," I heard our minister say last Sunday. His voice resounded through the church. He concluded, saying, "Don't put God in a box."

When we stood in line to shake his hand after church, I told him, "Marv's continued good health reminds me that God is not in a box. God is working outside of the box every day."

I experienced this last week when I visited my friends in Chicago. Marv did fine at home without me. Our daughter checked in and came over for the weekly hospice visit to take notes for me, and he finished his carpentry projects for our younger grandchildren.

Here I was on my own, nearly four months after Marv's diagnosis, in my old neighborhood in the Chicago Loop, seeing friends and staying at the Hyatt on Wacker with my longtime nursing friend, Marianna. My Fitbit told me that for the trip I walked a total of 49,504 steps, 41,559 more than the prior week. On the best day, I logged 15,472.

How fun it was to mingle again with the skyscrapers and honking horns on Michigan Avenue while feeling my thigh muscles wake up, contract, and cringe with every incline or set of stairs.

The best part was being with friends: spending a few hours with a former member of my writing group discussing our writing projects, kids, grandkids, and aging; another hour with a friend talking about her new, long-awaited grandchild; a long, long lunch with several friends sharing our innermost feelings about our lives today, the activities that keep us vital and on the go, and the challenges we face as we look forward. These friends and I go way back, and they are trusted confidants for me to unload the unique challenges I have now as Marv and I are living with the uncertainty of the progression of his small cell lung cancer.

Then there's Marianna. We met in the mid-1970s in a class we were taking toward completing our bachelor's degrees in nursing. As I wrote in my nursing career memoir, *Caring Lessons* (Deep River, 2010, p. 77):

> I first saw her red hair. Not ordinary red hair, but wild, bushy, like it was allergic to combs. Her eyes, piercing from under flyaway bangs, looked as if they'd seen Rome, London, Paris—places beyond my new life in Park Forest [Illinois]. . . . Her clothes—baggy jeans, plaid shirt, scuffed loafers—surprised me, a proud graduate of Stretch & Sew lessons.

We became friends that day, and we've been friends over the years through several moves, first around and now away from Chicago. This meet-up in Chicago had been planned before Marv's diagnosis. Afterward, I questioned whether I'd want to go so soon after Marv had died or if, perchance, he were still alive, he most certainly would be very ill. But neither of those things happened. Being able to go feels like another God thing— another instance of God's grace, another time of God acting outside the box.

Our husbands joke that, when we're together, Marianna and I talk nonstop. That's true. And, as my step counter proved, we also walked nearly nonstop on the days we spent with each other.

Even as sleet pelted our faces, we had to prove we were still young and hardy. We refused to take a cab to the Steppenwolf Theater to see Hershey Felder, pianist and composer, enact the life of *Our Great Tchaikovsky*. We chose to take the 'L,' which involved walking, at night, several blocks to the train and then to the theater, heads down, watching our feet so we wouldn't fall on the freezing slush forming ice patches on the uneven sidewalks, and then back again. That's April in Chicago. Topping off the evening, with a Bailey's for me and a Merlot for her, we lounged in the lobby of the Hyatt, just as if we stayed up till midnight every day in big cities having drinks in upscale hotels.

There was a long day of meandering north to the Ohio Street Yolk for breakfast, then east over to Navy Pier, then all 3,300 feet to the end of the Pier and back, and then a jaunt north to Water Tower Place. We stopped at an apartment complex and inquired about short-term rentals. I found my mind, even during these great times with friends, always wandering to, "What's next after Marv dies? How will I want to spend winters?" Warm-weather places without friends don't appeal to me, but will semi-hibernation in Sioux Falls snowstorms be a first choice? Or would Chicago, in a short-term rental, with familiarity and friends (and endless classes that I love) be a possibility?

I don't have answers yet, of course. But the opportunity to be with old friends and talking and walking and processing with Marianna, at exactly this time, was truly a gift.

CHAPTER THIRTEEN

April 30, 2018

Email

To: Marianna

Winding up some paperwork today in preparation for my putting in the edits on Marv's book. Getting a copy from the publisher. That will take at least a day or two this week.

Decided with business cards to present myself more as a creative nonfiction writer than as an author of a professional memoir. So picked out several designs and asked Marv's input. He chose one with random blue and yellow and pink hexagons on a black background. Creative!

We think Marv has another lump. Something is sprouting on his right temple beneath his hairline. He hopes it's not a horn. He maintains some humor!

Had fun laughs with my Phoenix friend with cancer who has lumps here and there. We decided we needed to live next door so we could have coffee and laugh every morning. She is the one who told me in January our visit was good for her because I make her laugh. I would add it's mutual. Since we were there, her husband discovered he had a localized cancer and had radiation. Fun and games.

Granddaughter Madison's girls' group at church had a program there last night. I met someone I knew. She wants to come over with her husband to pray with us. Nice gesture. We'll see what comes of it.

When people asked Marv at our church yesterday how he was doing, he said "good" with his jaw trembling and eyes tearing.

So another week begins. I'm back to my plateau weight, 157.8, after gaining again last week. I'm not walking, so that's my goal for this week. Marv's weight stays about the same, not losing or gaining.

Looking forward to a quiet evening. Feeling a tremendous sense of peace and gratitude that we're able to take care of all loose ends in a timely fashion. God is watching!

Blog Post

"I couldn't do what you're doing," we hear frequently, referring to my husband's decision to forgo cancer treatment. It's not been too hard so far because Marv's been "normal." But that changed last week when he sprouted his first new nodule since the one removed on January 23 that led to his diagnosis of Stage IV small cell lung cancer. He found the new nodule and asked me to check it. Sure enough, there is a firm and movable "marble" under the skin with no pain.

We've known all along the cancer is outside his lungs, traveling around and deciding where to land. In my mind, that landing would be internal, most likely in the bones or brain where lung cancer usually metastasizes, but here we are with a palpable bump on his forehead.

I didn't ask him until that evening how it felt to have external evidence of the progression of the disease. As we sat in our usual places in our living room—he in his recliner, me on the couch—he said he felt "nothing, really." I admitted I didn't either.

I wondered why I didn't react, and came up with the idea that I'm probably in some level of denial that the cancer is a reality. I recalled reading in Elizabeth Kubler-Ross's *On Death and Dying* about her stages of grief: denial, anger, bargaining, depression, and acceptance—stages that can occur in any order, not necessarily linearly.

When we learned of Marv's cancer in January, we were in some level of acceptance from the beginning. It did not come as a surprise; we'd had his lung scare in 2010, and he'd smoked since he was 15 (with so many attempts to quit, I long ago lost count). I never felt a need to bargain with God—"If only You do this, I'll do that"—and I've never felt depressed. Sad, yes, but not depressed in any clinical sense.

Early on, I did feel tremendously angry at tobacco manufacturers for making such an addictive product. However, I could not muster up any feeling of anger toward God and certainly not toward Marv.

I've lived with Marv's addiction during our courtship of three years and our marriage of fifty-five. I've seen him try to quit; I've seen his successful attempts for up to three months. But mostly I've seen how cigarettes and coffee have worked together to calm him. He has always been on the go. His mind is constantly creating innovative ideas, and his thoughts are usually larger in scope and miles ahead of anyone else in the room. A therapist we consulted once for Marv's "can't sit" state concluded, after extensive testing, that his brain is wired differently than about 80 percent of the rest of us. She assured us that being wired differently is okay; the world needs energetic, creative types like him. So do I wish he'd never smoked and maybe we wouldn't be here today? Of course, but I can't fault him for dealing with his "can't sit" personality with the thing that worked for him. I accept what he said right away upon diagnosis: "I'm not going to beat myself up for smoking; I know why I did it, and I don't expect others to understand."

Now, with this new nodule, our first external evidence since the diagnosis of the last one, I must confront the fact that the cancer is indeed real. Even though Marv is still running circles around me (he did three hours of yardwork the other day), I'll have to work on my level of denial. And I'll have to adjust my thinking very soon, as today we think there's another nodule starting to sprout.

May 5, 2018

Email

To: My Sisters

All is good here. Marv and I both had a busy week with odds and ends. Marv is hoping to finish the edits on his legacy book today, and proofing it is my next task. I have the original. If I can figure out the editing program, it seems easier for me to make my changes than to explain them all to the publisher, even though he is more than willing to help in any way. Marv wants to make some things clearer than when he was talking conversationally.

We are being positive and, for now, planning to come for the Grand Rapids wedding on June 9. I'm starting to work on those hotel arrangements soon.

Another God thing: one of my former nursing students in the Grand Rapids area is discussing my nursing book in her book club on June 9 and has invited me to attend. It's in the morning before the wedding—how amazing these both are on the same day in the same town. So I told Marv he has to make it until then, and he's going to try.

We will spend a day in Chicago on our way to Grand Rapids and will come home right after. Marv still feels fine and has not lost weight. Two great signs.

My blood pressure, on the other hand, is up. Running 150 systolic. It's usually in the 130s. I'm monitoring to see whether I should see my doctor. It's surely due to the stress hanging over our heads.

I'm planning to attend the Iowa Summer Writing Festival June 14–23. Jon and/or Sheri will come to be with Marv part of that time. Kath will cover if need be. They are insisting I care for myself. My writing friend from Chicago is going too, and we are taking the same two courses and staying at the same place. This was planned months ago when I thought I would be alone by now. Another God thing?

May 14, 2018

Email

To: Chicago Writing Friends

I'm going to use my blog posts of the cancer experience for my submission to the Iowa workshop. I hope to put those in book form someday. Writing helps ground me during this surreal waiting period.

I sold eight copies of *Caring Lessons* on Saturday (it's Nurses Week) at a Christian bookstore, and they sold six more that afternoon. Today, they asked for five more. Marv's glad to get rid of storing my last boxes.

Iowa—a month from Friday! Marv says he'll hold on so I can go without worrying. So far, he's good.

CHAPTER FOURTEEN

May 18, 2018

Blog Post

I feel more and more alone as the spouse of someone living with Stage IV small cell lung cancer who has chosen not to seek treatment. I've found no one whose spouse has made the same choice, so I have no one with whom to share my anxiety about when our "untreated" situation will change and what that change will look like.

Instead, I've submerged myself in the online places where persons live who are undergoing treatment for this same cancer. I've read countless stories about treatments, side effects, deteriorations, and deaths, as well as remissions—though temporary—and hope. I've felt surrounded in those stories by a huge dose of love, support, and encouragement for and from the many who have suffered the challenges of terminal cancer.

I remember when I required my nursing students to attend a support group of their choice during their mental health nursing practicum. I went to a few open meetings myself and recall feeling like I wanted to have my own "issue" because I loved the unconditional support offered in those meetings. I wanted to attend in a capacity other than as "the nursing students' teacher."

Now, I have a bona fide issue of my own! What if I found a support group with spouses in my exact situation? What might that look like?

For one thing, I would want lengthy conversations about why their spouses chose not to seek treatment and how their introduction into the world of cancer progressed. How did they find out they had cancer? What were their symptoms? Was their cancer discovered by default like my husband's? Then, what doctors did they see? Internist as gatekeeper? Pulmonologist for definitive diagnosis? Surgeon for biopsy? Oncologist to hear treatment options? And who else along the way?

And what did they hear from each one? Did they hear "a few weeks to a few months," "very aggressive," or "you must start treatment right away"?

Or did those doctors start out with, "What are your priorities? What's most important to you now?"

In my informal conversations with folks who have lived through other types of cancers, I ask how their doctor visits went. To a person, they went like ours; all health care workers, from receptionists to nurses to doctors, assumed they were there to seek treatment. Once, for us, a "before" photo was taken, and I wanted to ask, "Before what?" A schedule for chemo was laid out to us before Marv said, as nicely as he could, to either hold the spiel or make it quick because he wasn't going to take treatment anyway.

No one's first question was: "What are your priorities? What's most important to you now?"

In my reading, I find this approach is called the medicalization of illness in later life. We older people are not allowed to die naturally because, historically, doctors are taught to treat and cure. The health care system revolves around that philosophy. Most of us still don't question our doctors, and instead follow blindly whatever they say we must do.

I'd heard about Atul Gawande's *Being Mortal* (Picador, 2017) before Marv got cancer and was happy someone reminded me of it (another whopper of God's grace). I finished it the night before we met with the oncologist, the final doctor we saw in our medical parade.

Gawande argues that doctors could use a different approach. He paraphrases Susan Block, a palliative care specialist: "There is no single way to take people with terminal illness through the process, but there are some rules. . . . You sit down. You make time. You're not determining if they want treatment X versus treatment Y. You're trying to learn what's most important to them under the circumstances—so that you can provide information and advice on the approach that gives them their best chance of achieving it. The process requires as much listening as talking. If you are talking more than half the time, you're talking too much" (p. 182).

"You're trying to learn what's most important to them. . . ."

We did not feel that concern first off in our medical parade, except from Marv's internist on our first visit (who encouraged us to follow through on our plans to travel). After that, we were grateful to hear that concern and encouragement again on our first hospice visit. Now every week, our hospice nurse asks our plans, commends our activities, and makes sure we feel equipped to do whatever we want to do.

It's a relief to have her on our side. I can only hope that whenever people face a cancer diagnosis, they do not immediately panic but instead seek out a doctor who asks, first, about their priorities. Someone who asks, "What is most important to you?" before the receptionist takes a picture or someone presents a treatment schedule.

And now, would you believe it? A few hours ago, I found a person online whose loved one was recently diagnosed with Stage IV small cell lung cancer, and they've found out it is too advanced for any treatment and have been referred to hospice. I reached out to them in support of hospice as a comforting measure and with an expression of prayer, and I've heard back.

I believe I've found a "support group" after all—a niche where I can support others when treatment is not possible and dying naturally becomes a life they didn't choose.

May 25, 2018

Notes

Today, Marv's publisher came over to videotape us about our experience. I'll never forget this day. The publisher, Jeremy, brought an assistant who worked the camera. Marv and I sat at our counter-height kitchen table, side by side. Jeremy sat across from us. Sunshine from the patio door cast a glow across the table. There was no sound except for the low, measured voices of the three of us; the quiet felt sacred. Marv looked perky in a pink-and-white long-sleeved shirt with cuffs rolled up. I, on the other hand, wore a gray linen shirt over a black shell. I didn't know I looked as tired as my shirt was drab until we got the video. I thought I was holding up well, but my fatigue must have been weighing on me more than I realized. I felt like we were playing a game of musical chairs, hopping feverishly from chair to chair but knowing that one day the music would stop and one person would no longer have a chair.

Marv started the interview, voice breaking. "Since we got the diagnosis, our life has been very, very special together. You get up in the morning—you say, 'Thank you, I'm here,' but you don't know the next day that you're gonna be back." The interview lasted about an hour. Toward the end, Marv repeated his motto: "There's no such word as 'can't.'" He always saw the glass as half-full compared to my view of half-empty. He added, "Believe in yourself. Have confidence. And you can make a difference."

Reviewing the video, I see the love in Marv's eyes as he included me in his responses. He even gave a plug for my blog and my book, saying, "If you really want to read about this recent journey . . . what do you call it?" I answered with the working title for this book at that time, "Grace Notes: Living with Untreated Small Cell Lung Cancer." He added, "I think it will be very, very beneficial for those who are facing a similar type of diagnosis."

At one point, he stopped talking and leaned over to give me a quick kiss. He had captured our mood, the day-to-day uncertainty and love between a couple married almost fifty-six years. My sadness caught in my throat.

May 28, 2018

Email

To: Marv's Siblings

With great joy, we are planning to attend a wedding on June 9 of a grandniece of mine in Allendale, Michigan. We never thought this would be possible, and we are very grateful. Marv continues to feel well. Except for a new lump along his jawline, which in the best-case scenario (but not likely) could be a swollen gland, he has no obvious symptoms.

So we will leave here Monday, June 4, get to Chicago on June 5, and stay till Thursday, June 7. We'll drive to Grand Rapids the morning of June 7, stay till Sunday morning, July 10, and then head home. Marv wants to drop in on all of you in Grand Rapids to give you a copy of his book.

This is not Farewell Hug Tour #2. It is truly a Tour of Gratitude to God.

May 29, 2018

Blog Post

There are moments that the seriousness and the certainty and the finality of our situation slam into my consciousness and I weep. The weeping only lasts for a moment, but I wonder what will happen after Marv is gone. Will I weep oceans? He continually reminds me, "You'll do fine." Big deal. What does he know? But I must admit his confidence in me is reassuring.

This past week, he finally taught me how to change the furnace filter—it had been on our bucket list. I also learned about the water softener. It's there, it has a lid, and I'm supposed to scoop stuff from a fifty-pound bag into it every now and then. I don't remember.

I don't want to dwell on the things I must know to be a widow. I said so to a few widow friends. They laughed and said, "We can teach you those things, Lois. Don't sweat the small stuff."

Helpful, for sure, but they don't realize, at my stage, these household maintenance things are a big deal. It almost makes me want to move into an apartment with a round-the-clock maintenance staff. Just when I voice my fears about the house falling apart, a neighbor offers up her husband. "He'll help you with everything, Lois. Just call. He loves to help."

I'm reading Joan Chittister's *The Gift of Years: Growing Older Gracefully* (BlueBridge, 2008) for a new book club we've started at church. All of us are loving the book. We're taking a third at a time and never finish the whole section because each person can relate to so many of the truisms the author says about aging. Last night I was reading the chapter titled, "Future"—a weird topic for me right now since my future is so uncertain. But right off, the opening sentence cheered me up. Chittister quoted Louis Kronenberger: "Old age is an excellent time for outrage. My goal is to say or do one outrageous thing a week" (p. 139).

"There you have it," as my older sister Rose likes to say. Chittister reminds us that the future is just a state of mind. We can either go negative with it or positive. But you sure get the feeling from her that life is now and that we should spend our time well, even dangerously: "Dangerously fun-loving, dangerously honest. Dangerously involved. Dangerously alive" (p. 161).

So I will tell Marv tonight that we must do something outrageous—even dangerous!

But today he's already washed the cars, planted more flowers, and worked on bedside tables he's making for our adult grandson. He has yet to make me dinner. He may say that's outrageous and dangerous enough for one day.

I will have to agree—outrageously and dangerously thoughtful and loving for that little-girl part of me that's a teeny bit afraid of becoming a widow.

May 30, 2018

Email

To: My Sisters

Talked with hospice today about where to put the hospital bed. Oh, so sobering. I'm glad our nurse is a planner too. I like to plan, as then I feel some sense of control.

June 4, 2018

Blog Post

We are taking time off from cancer. Well, not really. But we've been pleasantly distracted with a few-day visit from friends from Arizona. While they were here, we visited Pipestone National Monument in Pipestone, Minnesota, about an hour from our home.

From the monument's website: "For countless generations, American Indians have quarried the red pipestone found at this site. These grounds are sacred to many people because the pipestone quarried here is carved into pipes used for prayer. Many believe the pipe's smoke carries one's prayer to the Great Spirit. The traditions of quarrying and pipe-making continue here today."

The warm and breezy day contributed to a sense of well-being and thankfulness for God's gifts of nature, Native American culture, and our lives, as we ambled along a three-quarter-mile trail.

This week, we're looking forward to another road trip to see family and friends—our Gratitude to God tour. It's now been five months since the initial PET scan warning. We are grateful for each added breath and each extra day.

If you see us sailing by on I-90 or I-94 or I-96, wave a hello!

Notes

Happy distractions are imperative when dealing with the uncertainty of dying. Some days, as if constantly *not-knowing-when* isn't enough, I have to turn off the national news. It seems there's a never-ending barrage of shootings, political upheaval, and climate disasters. I feel like my mind is too crowded to handle one more thing. When I get ready for bed, I find myself humming a Sunday School song: "Why worry when you can pray?" So I add my concerns for my country, and for the world, to my personal fears and turn them over to God in prayer.

In Retrospect

Remembering the warm and comforting period of our travels, I see how Marv's insistence on making these farewell trips and driving those miles enabled him to patch together the relationships and experiences that were meaningful in his life. To interact again with family, friends, and colleagues supported his belief that he'd reached, in Erik Erikson's *Childhood and Society* developmental stage theory, the eighth stage of ego integrity versus despair. Marv's rationale went like this: "If I hadn't reached ego integrity—that is, if I'd not accomplished everything I wanted to do in life and felt good about it—if I had any regrets about my life, I'm not so sure I'd have been able to make the decision to refuse treatment."

CHAPTER FIFTEEN

June 8, 2018

Notes

The wedding day tomorrow is sure to be beautiful, but I have some anxiety about a huge gathering. I'm remembering a time soon after Marv's diagnosis when I lost it, and I don't want a repeat.

In planning Marv's visits back in February, I thought everything was going as well as could be expected considering the rationale. But at one gathering, when I heard a raised voice in the next room, I could tell that the ruckus was being directed at Marv.

I snapped. I flew into the room and went to stand next to him. Then I heard myself screaming, "I'm going to be a widow soon, and I need everyone to get along!"

To this day I can't believe that came out of my mouth. The words ricocheted around the room. Someone told me later, "I've never seen you that angry. Your mama bear really came out." I was totally unaware that underneath my calm exterior, I was a powder keg of stress just waiting to explode.

Thankfully, the situation resolved quickly. Marv didn't take anything personally. As a social worker, he has always felt that getting through bad stuff is necessary and healthy to get to the other side. An outburst couldn't faze him, other than the compassion he felt for anyone's suffering. He didn't say anything about my heroics/

hysterics either; he just accepted what I'd done and loved me just the same.

Now it's time to see family and friends again. I pray that God's grace will be there with us.

June 9, 2018

In Retrospect

June 9, 2018, is forever in my memory. It was the day of both the book club event and the family wedding. And the day was so filled with grace.

It was definitely a grace thing to attend that book club meeting as their author guest—just what I needed as a break from all the family visits focused on farewells. My former student, Micky, picked me up at the hotel where Marv and I were staying and drove us to the host's home. It was great catching up. When one is so entrenched in the trajectory of dying, it's easy to forget that other people's lives continue.

The host and the other women greeted me warmly, which made me feel like a celebrity. The host had set a bright, summery table and served muffins, an egg bake, and fresh fruit. I hadn't expected such a spread, and the ambience in a home overlooking a lake was a real upper. Each attendee, all health care professionals like Micky, had come prepared with a question to ask, and the meeting evolved into a stimulating discussion among the nine of us. I felt so much affirmation for my book. And, I realized later, it was an important time to just be me, in my own identities of nurse and writer, which gave me a respite from my caregiver role.

The wedding, too, that afternoon was an upper. It was held outside in a rural setting. A red barn served as the backdrop for the couple's vows. Marv and I sat in the second row on the bride's side. I sensed that he, seeing that barn, was reliving childhood memories. His facial expression said he was clearly happy to be here. Before and after the ceremony he mingled among the guests. This wedding was on my side of the family, so it gave Marv a chance to see more of the Hoitenga relatives. His posture showed the enthusiasm of someone who thought he would live forever. A bystander could not have guessed his life was coming to a close.

At the reception afterward, held in the barn, Marv especially enjoyed dances with a few nieces. I watched from the sidelines, marveling at his stamina and will to live. Others came by and wished us well. It was good to share some time with my sister-in-law, the bride's grandmother Kay. Her husband, my brother Dewey, had died in 2005. It was sobering to think I, too, would soon be attending my grandchildren's special events alone.

June 24, 2018

Blog Post

We took off for Chicago and Michigan on June 4. We were gone eight days, drove 1,700 miles, and had made fifteen stops. I'm getting pretty good at scheduling these marathon trips. Marv drove all but one hour, and we saw many friends and family.

The main prompt for the trip was my grandniece's wedding near Grand Rapids, Michigan, on June 9. I'd told her I couldn't RSVP because of the uncertainty of our situation, but she said to come if we could; they'd hold a place for us. It was a grand reunion of some of my Hoitenga relatives; my grandniece is my brother Dewey's grandchild.

A highlight in Chicago was staying at the Heritage, our former condo building near Michigan and Randolph overlooking

Millennium Park. Seeing friends there and getting hugs from our doormen were special treats. It seemed like we'd left there yesterday, rather than already two years ago.

We were home only three days from our marathon trip when I left again. Way last March (three months ago), when Marv's days seemed numbered, he'd encouraged me to sign up for the Iowa Summer Writing Festival. Our thinking was that he'd be gone and this happy place of mine—it'd be my tenth summer to attend— would be a good thing to have on my calendar. So now, with his booting me out, our son from Seattle flying in to spend some time with him, and our daughter covering the rest of the time, I drove my Beetle to Iowa City (a six-hour trip) and took a weekend course on metaphors and a week-long course on blending our personal memoir stories within the broader context of societal concerns. For example, Marv's refusal to undergo chemo is in sync now with the movement for, as is said in Gawande's *Being Mortal* and other current literature, "dying naturally," the notion of less medicalization of aging-related diseases.

And, as he had promised, Marv hung in the entire week I was away. I called him every morning to see how he was. Every day he answered the same: "I'm fine." Then he'd follow with something like, "Are you having a good time?" His voice sounded strong and good, and I had no reason to suspect that anything was changing.

Midweek, Marv sent me an article from *The New York Times* by Jason B. Rosenthal entitled, "My Wife Says You May Want to Marry Me" (June 5, 2018). Rosenthal wrote the article in response to his wife's article the year prior when she gave him permission, as she was dying, to keep on living and, among other things, to marry again. In my phone call that day to Marv, he said, "I feel the same way for you." He often said that he was the one who was dying, not me, and I must go on living a full life. "Thank you, honey," was the best response I could muster up as my voice cracked, and then I added, "but I'd rather have you."

I arrived home in Sioux Falls at four yesterday, June 23. Marv was *very* happy to have me home again, and I am *very* happy to be home and will be home now for the duration. He is seeing some changes; the disease is clearly progressing. Today, we are working on his obituary and the program for his memorial service. As usual, I'm sitting here at my desk while he dictates his wishes and his preferred wording to me. Then I will send a copy to his computer so he can tell me what I missed or give me the go-ahead. We are a team! Between his more frequent needs for naps and pain control, we'll get the necessary work done.

And would you believe it? He asked me to take a walk around the block earlier. I've been after him for years, no exaggeration, to take a walk with me. We strolled around our block. He said, "You sure picked out a nice neighborhood." A fun compliment since he'd sent me here to buy the house by myself (with our daughter's help, of course!).

Now, our daughter and family are dropping in. Our son and daughter-in-law called earlier from their car, en route home to Seattle from a weekend away.

Tomorrow, Marv will finish making, as requested, a coffee table for our adult grandson who lives nearby. We are truly blessed!

Notes

Kathleen told me she didn't want Marv to mow their lawn anymore. Last week Wednesday, when I was in Iowa, he'd gone over to her house to mow the lawn. The grandkids love to ride on the mower with him. Kath snapped pictures, wondering if this would be the last time as she'd noticed he was unsteady walking. Then when he returned from their large backyard and came around to the front of the house, with the kids sitting on the front of the mower, he'd not stopped in time and crashed into something in the driveway.

That was a first. But I cannot imagine Marv giving up his beloved rides on the John Deere.

A Memory from Jon

I flew out to stay with Dad for five days while Mom was gone to Iowa. Kath had scheduled a massage for him. I was not comfortable with Dad driving, so I directed him to the passenger side. But he would not give up the electronic key fob. No problem, as he just had to be near me for me to start the car. We stopped on the way at a gas station so Dad could buy cigarettes. When we got to the massage place, Dad insisted I did not need to escort him into the building. So I just watched him go in and drove off to have coffee somewhere while I waited. A few miles away, the dashboard lit up telling me that the key fob was not in range. Well, it had stayed in Dad's pocket! What was I to do? I was closer to home by then, so hoped I'd make it. The engine stopped as I drove up the driveway. I made sure I took a second fob on all further adventures with Dad!

PART IV

THE CHANGE

CHAPTER SIXTEEN

Monday, June 25, 2018

Email

To: Marv's Siblings

We need your prayers. Marv started having slight headaches last week, but they became unbearable over the weekend. He has not been successful with pain relief. He now has horrendous, debilitating pressure behind his eyes. Our hospice nurse is coming in an hour.

Email

To: My Sisters

Sara (hospice nurse) was here. Usually comes on Wednesday. Marv called her. She noted worsening headache, leg pains, and a balance issue. Starting on routine morphine for pain and steroids for pain and inflammation. He is napping now. Sara forbade carpentry work today! No saws! She is off tomorrow but will send someone else. Hospice will deliver the new meds to our house. All good at the moment. I'm skipping our church book club this morning.

Email

To: My Sisters [later]

Marv in bed. Headache 0/10! Thank God. On morphine 15 mg every 4 hours. Can have 30 mg every 2 hours. Slept three hours this morning, then three hours again after lunch. Threw up. Had felt sick all day, even before morphine.

We went to get milk and Chinese for dinner at our grocery store. Marv had three bites. Felt sick and quit. Unsteady on his feet. Hoping morphine relieves pain in legs too.

Came home to hospice (Avera@Home) in our driveway delivering meds (morphine, Dexamethasone—steroid for inflammation and pain, and Senna-S). The man was so kind that I broke down sobbing as he left. Sara, the hospice nurse, called minutes later to confirm delivery. More tears. The Avera logo on the delivery man's car is a cross and upstretched hands. We feel so cared for.

I got many comforting notes today. Feeling grateful. I think we have now reached the drop-off we were told would happen— Marv would go full tilt until he doesn't. The "doesn't" seems to have happened. Marv feels it too.

I wrote a draft of the memorial program today. Marv was going to help, but the few minutes he was awake he was working on our grandson's coffee table. Our pastor, David Halleen, comes home tomorrow from a two-week vacation. Marv called the church office today to request a visit on Wednesday. I want to have a draft of the program ready for him. I followed the format of sister Kay's memorial and that of a woman from our church who just died: "A Celebration Service of the Resurrection of Christ and of the Life of Marvin D. 'Marv' Roelofs."

Sobering. Unreal.

Two friends from Chicago are planning to come for the memorial, so I got their availability. Jon and Sheri are going to Iceland and Kath and Michael to South Haven, Michigan, in July, so I will work a memorial around their absences and the availability of our pastor, soloist, and organist. Hopefully it can be on a Saturday around one, so Marv's hometown folks can make it in a day.

He's still here with us, and I'm trying to schedule the funeral.

Good night and thanks for being there for me today. Am so thankful for prayers, hospice, and morphine. Everything is surreal.

Tuesday, June 26, 2018

Email

To: My Sisters

After waking up for meds at eleven, Marv slept all night (after having gone to bed around seven). Thankful.

Hospice here this morning. New gal. No more driving or sawing for Marv since he's on morphine. She sat with us like she had all the time in the world.

Later, emergency delivery of more meds. Marv napping. More tears from me. Delivery person said, "God bless," after hearing our story. I choked up as he left. I don't think I'll ever forget the hopeful image of that Avera car on our driveway.

Nurse Sara called, checking that we got meds. It's her day off. Amazing.

Marv unsteady and dizzy and nauseated when up. He says he might as well take advantage of being able to nap and generally tells people he's "good," but things are changing. He had fun phone calls this morning with a Chicago friend and with one of his sisters.

Looking forward now to Jon coming all next week and all of us hopefully making it to Marv's hometown of Prinsburg, Minnesota, for one last July 4 celebration with lots of family and friends.

I have writing work to do, left over from Iowa. Nice distraction. Quiet here.

Notes

Evening.

This has been a mind-blowing day.

Marv told me that during his morning nap he'd seen three friends hovering around the bed. During his afternoon nap, he'd seen Chinese people in the bedroom. As he told me about these things, we were a little silly about it. Who would show up next? I wasn't alarmed at the first instance because we knew those people—I thought maybe he was dreaming. But after the story about the Chinese, I called hospice. Could the hallucinations be related to the medication? The nurse gave me instructions to cut back on morphine and said she'd reassess tomorrow.

Later that afternoon, Marv reported he saw "two mirages" while he was sitting outside and smoking. Otherwise, he was alert and coherent. He seemed nonchalant about seeing things that weren't there. I think we were both more curious than afraid. We took a walk around the block after dinner. Marv talked with neighbors. He was "with it" all evening.

We went to bed around eleven. We were talking and the lights were out when he said, "What's that cat doing on your shoulder?"

It was too dark; there was no way he could have seen anything on my shoulder, even if something were there. "Honey, there is no cat on my shoulder. We don't even have a cat."

"Why are you standing on my side of the bed?"

"I'm not. I am right next to you, on your left side, as always."

"There's a large cobweb hanging over us." He gestured broadly toward the ceiling as he outlined the dimensions of the web. "There's a girl in bed with us. She has long blond braids."

By that time, while it was still a bit comical, I was getting concerned. "Honey, if we called Kathleen right now and told her you saw a cat on my shoulder, she'd think we'd really gone Looney Tunes."

"Call her."

It was quarter after eleven, so I thought she'd still be awake. I told her Dad had seen a cat on my shoulder and handed the phone to Marv and had him tell her too. He was alert while telling her the story and sounded as though he thought he was speaking gospel truth. I put the phone on speaker while we told her the other things Marv was seeing. Her response was silence. I think she was incredulous her folks were being so silly at that late hour. As we hung up, we promised her we'd let her know if anyone, or anything, else showed up during the night.

At 12:15 a.m., I sensed Marv getting up, probably needing to go to the bathroom. The only light in our room, adjacent to the bathroom, were two nightlights in wall outlets, barely enough to light a path to the bathroom. I felt him groping around the foot of the bed and opened my eyes to find him stuck in the corner between my side of the bed and the bathroom. I bolted out of bed and guided him into the bathroom.

Back in bed, I waited for him. When he came out, I turned on the reading light over my side of the bed and guided him back to his side. He said he'd thrown up in the bathroom. He said he smelled cement and dirt. As he sat on his side of the bed, he motioned toward our backyard: "Someone's working on our patio." The wooden blinds were closed. No way could he see anyone out there, plus no one would be out there at that time of night. He seemed oblivious to these incongruities.

I didn't contradict him anymore. It was clear that he was really starting to hallucinate. I didn't know what that meant yet, but I got my little notebook out to start documenting. I would want to tell the nurse all the details in the morning.

We lay quietly until 12:40. With his eyes closed, Marv suddenly announced, "The sheets are all red and bloody. Someone is dancing on your right shoulder. Jacob and Madison [our grandkids] are out there somewhere. I want to sleep." He had been on his back and turned toward me. "I have to face you, because I can't face the window." He described seeing "purplish strings with green leaves." He flipped back on his right side and got up. "I have to get a Pop Tart to settle something down."

I turned my reading light on again, so he could see to get up to go to the kitchen. I heard him rustle around in the kitchen getting a Pop Tart. I got up and peeked around the corner to the kitchen to make sure he was okay.

When he came back, he said, "Whatever you do, I'm not going to the emergency room." I said nothing, not sure of what was on his mind, as he slid back into bed. "Turn the light off," he said. "I want to sleep."

At 12:50, he said, sounding like a reporter, "There is sand blowing. Red sand, blowing all over. I know it's not real." I reassured him it wasn't real.

At 1:10, he got up to go to the bathroom. I switched on the light and watched him grope his way around the bed into the bathroom. On his way back, he said, "Are we moving? In a cage. All a mess. Dowels. People walking all over."

Each time he awakened, I stayed calm, alert to ensure he stayed safe. There was no sense calling hospice now. What would they do at that hour of the night? I reasoned that if his behavior did not threaten my safety or his, I could go into nurse mode and chart what I was observing. I sort of detached from him as my husband then and observed him clinically, as if he were my patient and I was responsible for documenting his behavior in the nurse's notes in his chart.

At 1:40, he was up again. Gagging. Said, "I'm very sick." He made some coffee in the microwave and sat in the garage, next to the open side door, to have a cigarette. I followed him to make sure he was settled, then lay on the couch, thinking I would hear him more easily when he tried to get back into the house.

At 2:00, he came back in, saw me on the couch and told me to go to bed. He said he'd stay on the couch. I left him on the couch with a standing lamp lit to its dimmest setting.

At 4:00, he came back to bed and slept until 5:15. I felt him trying to sort out the comforter, blanket, and sheet. I opened my eyes to see him throwing the linens up over his head. I asked if he needed help. He said, "I need these over my head, so I don't see all the red stuff." He was soon up and groping to find the door to the hallway. I asked where he was going. He answered, "All angles." I turned on the light, and he was oriented and lucid again.

At 6:00, he was back on the couch, gesturing toward the ceiling. "What are those plates doing up there? A guy was working on the wire that hooked up to the fan. Something big on top of the fan there. Don't you see it?" I was sitting in a recliner nearby, writing my notes, and when I didn't answer right away, he said, "I take it you don't see any red in the ceiling. A lot of red."

I said, "No, I don't see it, but I can understand that it looks real to you."

At 6:30, the hospice nurse called in response to my call a half hour earlier. I gave her my report. She said they'd discuss Marv at their team meeting that morning. She told me to hold all medications. I told her also that Marv had said, when he was outside during the night, that a plant normally in the ground was on the sidewalk by the garage. And he'd seen a lizard catch a cricket, and two crickets had come to drag the dead cricket away.

From 8:00 to 9:00, Marv slept in bed. When he woke up, he said he'd seen children eating breakfast all around the room. Now that he was awake, he saw the mess they'd left in the room.

At 10:15, he was sitting in his recliner, looking across the room at the fireplace. "There are blue and white threads in the carpeting." I said, "Where? I don't see them." He insisted they were there. He got up and retrieved a dustpan and brush from the laundry room. He knelt on all fours and brushed the nonexistent threads into the dustpan.

As I sat by watching, exhausted, tears seeped from my eyes. This was no longer anything silly; something serious was happening to Marv's brain. My whole body felt slammed by the starkness of the reality that was right before my eyes—I was losing the husband I knew. The intelligent, rational guy who could always answer my questions, whether he knew the answer or not, was leaving me— the guy who'd diapered our kids, driven them to orthodontia, discussed issues with them as teens at our supper table. I thought to quickly snap a picture. He was on his hands and knees. So very sad.

He stood and came over to show me the dustpan. "Do you see them now?" I did see a few teeny white flecks. Our carpeting has blue and white and tan threads in a muted tweed pattern. I took another picture. *Could it be his brain is so hyper-alert that he can see the teeny individual white threads?*

Wednesday, June 27, 2018

Notes

The strange thing about the night of the advent of hallucinations was that between episodes Marv was lucid and rational. It was like, "Who's on first?" Was he for real or was he joking? He had a dry sense of humor and some of things he said could have been to pull my leg. But he was too serious for him to be joking. That was even more sobering. I waited anxiously all morning to hear the report from the hospice staff meeting.

At 2:00 p.m., hospice came. Sara our regular nurse, and the social worker Kelly, reported on the team meeting. They feel there is metastasis from the lung to the frontal lobe of the brain. The recent symptoms of Marv's unsteady gait and increasing headaches, and now the sudden onset of hallucinations, all point to brain involvement. Sara outlined medication changes to address this new problem, primarily a steroid to reduce brain inflammation and an anti-seizure medication.

During the night of hallucinations, I hadn't even thought of the possibility of seizures. My goodness. Here I had thought I'd handled the situation so well, not getting riled up, calmly observing and taking notes, trying to be the reliable caregiver I'd hoped I would be. I quickly consoled myself that if Marv would have had a seizure, my training as a nurse would have reappeared: turn the patient on his side, make sure he doesn't aspirate. Sara went on to say if Marv does have a seizure, I must immediately get the Lorazepam from the Comfort Kit in the refrigerator and give him doses every fifteen minutes times three. While hospice care is not about the patient getting cured, it is paramount that the patient be as comfortable as possible through the process.

Then Kelly told me about different caregiver agencies in Sioux Falls. Clearly, I could not care for Marv if he were not sleeping and I could not get sleep. She recommended one agency that some of her former clients had liked; they charged between $20 and $25 an hour. I instantly computed: an overnight shift, eleven to seven, could cost about $200, which would be worth it for a good night's sleep. But then I found out that they didn't give medications. That wouldn't work. Only I would know what medications to give Marv and when to give them through the night as he became restless.

The social worker also reminded me I could have home health aides up to ten hours a week and two hours a day. I could ask them to do little things around the house. All I could think of then, after that whole night without sleep, was that I wanted to sleep for a week. She suggested I could get a baby monitor if that would help me sleep, say, out on the couch. Of course, that wouldn't work either. With Marv's unsteadiness and possible disorientation during the night, I'd have to be there to sense any movement and act quickly for his safety.

Email

To: All Family

The sudden change in Marv's condition we were told would happen has happened. All in a few days, Marv developed an unsteady gait, a severe headache behind his eyes, and starting yesterday, hallucinations. The hospice team discussed him today and, with these latest symptoms, diagnosed the presence of a growing mass in the frontal part of his brain. Our nurse and social worker came together today to break the news. We were hoping the hallucinations were simply caused by a medication reaction. It may be weeks before his death, but since the brain is involved, it will likely be sooner than if the new symptoms involved other organs.

Marv took the news pragmatically and plans to finish the coffee table he's building for Kyle and Kaileen, who are marrying near here August 18.

Our pastor came this afternoon, and we presented the obituary and memorial service we'd prepared over the weekend. He loved that we did all the work! While he was here, Marv pointed out a red worm crawling across the carpet that, of course, was not there. (I read this letter over to Marv, and he said with a chuckle to tell you it was there! So there!)

After the pastor left, Marv heated up leftovers, served me as usual, and did dishes. The brain is fascinating in how it works—one second here, the next second light years away.

For his safety, I am not to leave him alone. Kathleen and I are discussing coverage for nights. I do need sleep! There are services where I can hire night coverage, but I want to wait to see if the new meds keep him asleep. Know that our faith is strong and we are enormously grateful for the last six months we've had together. Marv got his wish for a super quality of life free from chemo. God is good! We've experienced simply oodles and oodles of God's grace. And we are now able to have some chuckles about all the new "guests" and "oddities" showing up in our house.

The sun is shining, the air is clear, and Marv just pointed out that it's raining. So interesting. And he's just served me his homemade rhubarb crisp with ice cream.

Thursday, June 28, 2018

Notes

Luckily, last night, Marv slept from eight until four. Today, while trying to finish the coffee table for Kyle, he could not figure out the angles of the legs. The top of the coffee table was completed, and it was upside-down on sawhorses. He'd wanted to angle the legs and, even after several cuts, could not get them correct to have the table be level.

I watched, not able to help. He was silent, not showing his frustration, but I could see it by his scribblings and drawings during his several coffee and cigarette breaks. Once, he said, "I can't figure out why it's not working." I thought of the dozens of things he's made for me and our kids—from bookshelves to end tables to swing sets. He'd never had computational problems before. I wondered how he felt, but I didn't ask. I felt an obligation to not worsen the situation. I wasn't sure he'd even comprehend that changes were going on in his brain.

I started a regular medication chart, set up for a week's worth of charting. I'd been charting Marv's meds on my daily notes, but now there were so many, with so many different times, that even I, a nurse, was getting mixed up. I thought, *How do lay people handle all this medication instruction?* I made columns in my little notebook, dating from 6/28 to 7/6 across the top, and listed the medications and times to be administered down the left hand column: Senexon-S, two tabs twice a day as laxative; Dexamethazone 4 mg twice a day for brain swelling; Levetiracetam 500 mg, twice a day as anti-seizure; morphine ER 15 mg at bedtime for pain; Haldol 0.5 mg, as needed to calm and at bedtime; morphine 15 mg as needed for pain; Lorazepam 0.5 mg as needed for seizure; Miralax one dose as needed for laxative. I left a few lines to add medications over that week, and then I added, like I'd done in nursing charting, a row to keep track of bowel movements as self-reported, urinary output as self-reported, confusion episodes, and presence of hallucinations.

When I finished composing the chart, my shoulders relaxed. I could see what I had to do and when. I'd set up all the medications on the top of my dryer by resurrecting a small three-tiered spice rack that held about twelve bottles, so I had my homemade medication shelving.

With Marv's definite change in condition, I thought to call the funeral home to give them a heads-up. It's weird what goes through your mind at a time like this. If I was thinking of what I felt were weird things, what was I missing at the same time?

The funeral director we'd set up our plans with shortly after we'd moved to Sioux Falls—just in case—thanked me for calling and said, "Hang in there, kiddo." What was I? A teen? I did get a chuckle out of the comment though. Me, at 76, a kiddo, caretaking her dying husband. So unreal.

CHAPTER SEVENTEEN

Friday, June 29, 2018

Blog Post

Our situation has changed. We'd been told Marv's condition could quickly get worse and now, in the past week, it has.

First, I'd like to share with you the following note that I wrote to my online support group for people who are living with Stage IV small cell lung cancer. After a summary of Marv's condition so far, I wrote: "We are so thankful for these six normal months from this known, very aggressive cancer, and we have received tons of support and prayers from our family and friends. We are at peace and pray for the same for each of you in your unique situations. Now we've been told his future is more limited, and we hope to live each remaining day to its fullest with the help of the first medications he's taken. I so appreciate the support I've seen here and each of you and your stories. Thanks for reading ours!"

I also thank you, my blog readers, for following what I feel are my Grace Notes, one after another of positive things that have happened for us since Marv's diagnosis. I'm thankful to report today that his new symptoms are under control, thanks to daily visits and medication help from hospice.

Today, we hung out at our daughter's garage sale, an annual event. This weekend our son and daughter-in-law fly in for the week. We plan another trip next week to celebrate the Fourth with family in the town where Marv grew up. Every day is precious, and we remain grateful!

Saturday, June 30, 2018

Notes

Marv had a massage this morning. He loves his massage therapist. He said, "She found all the tight spots again—the muscles in my legs causing the cramps." No bowel movements today but four yesterday. We celebrate each one. Being on morphine, known to cause constipation, he can't afford to get plugged up. He worked on the legs for the coffee table again and still couldn't get them cut right. He won't wait for Jon, who's flying in tonight. He enjoyed new phone calls from a sister and another Chicago friend. A neighbor brought dinner—seven-layer salad, sloppy joes, pineapple cake. Such a nice gesture.

Sunday, July 1, 2018

Notes

Jon here. All to church. Kath and family joined us and came for dinner. We had plenty of leftovers from what the neighbor brought last night. With Jon here, I could skip out for a while and not worry. Went to the mall. Bought a bright floral dress for the funeral service. Marv warned me once, "Don't wear black. Wear something happy. It will be a happy occasion." I did not show him when I came home. What would I have said? We'd talked about so much, but showing him my dress seemed to cross a line. I could not bring myself to say,

"Look, honey, I found the happy dress you suggested I get for your funeral." I was glad, however, that I had found something. One less thing to worry about. And I know he might have said, with his usual smile at my purchases, "Great—now I know I can pass away at any time."

Monday, July 2, 2018

Notes

Hospice nurse Sara is here. Marv's usual slight hand tremors are worse, maybe due to the changes in the brain. The new brain medications seem to be helping, since there have been no more hallucinations.

Wednesday, July 4, 2018

Notes

Sheri flew in yesterday. She and Jon drove us to Prinsburg for the town's annual holiday celebration.

We arrived just before a rainstorm, the patriotic service in church just letting out. We hustled into the school gym for the barbecued-pork lunch. Kathleen and family had driven separately, but we were all in line together.

I lost Marv right away. He found old acquaintances in the line, then in the gym where tables were filling up. Jon, Sheri, and I were almost finished eating before Marv showed up with his plate. He said later that he'd talked to about fifty people and he'd never had such a good time. Got many hugs. It was good to see him so happy.

During the annual parade down Main Street, a group of relatives were lined up in Marv's sister's front yard. I glanced down the row to find him. I noticed his legs had a yellowish cast. I asked Sheri, "Do Dad's legs look yellow?" She turned to look. "Yes," she said, frowning.

I hadn't noticed a color change before. Was it the late afternoon sun? Was it because he was wearing a new bright yellow T-shirt? My nurse mind answered automatically, "Maybe liver. The cancer's gone to his liver." I asked a nurse cousin what she thought. "Liver," she replied.

I don't know why, but this new development did not register as serious. It felt as though my new observation hit me, then slid right off as if I were smeared in butter. I think I must have been too tired and too numb to register anything new.

A Memory from Jon

One of my fondest memories of the last trip to Prinsburg was seeing Dad light up being "home." It was the Fourth of July. Everyone in Prinsburg and the surrounding area was there—probably all 826 of them. (The town's population is around 500.) It seemed like Dad knew everyone. He did not lose steam throughout the day. He, in his yellow shirt, loved talking to everyone. This was a delight to watch. Sheri reminded me afterward that Kathleen was busy taking pictures for Dad's memorial service. That's Kath, always thinking ahead.

Friday, July 6, 2018

Notes

After the parade in Prinsburg, we stayed at a Willmar hotel, twenty minutes away. In the morning, Marv told me, "I had an awful night.

Was up several times. Had tight, rope-like pain in my legs. Like cramps."

"Where'd you go?"

"Outside. In front. At a table. Smoked. Had coffee."

Local cousins joined us in the breakfast room. Marv didn't let on that he was in pain. It was hard to see him hug these people goodbye. Long, snug hugs. All knew it would be the last time. Then Jon and Sheri drove us two hours north to brother Rog's cottage.

We've always loved this trip to visit them. After lunch, they offered a pontoon ride as usual. The day was perfect, with blue skies, warm breezes, and calm waters. We circled the lake. We were gone over an hour. Our plan was to have dinner, stay overnight, and leave for home in the morning.

As soon as we got off the boat, Marv came to me on the lawn in front of the cottage. "I need to go home."

I didn't understand. He had not let on anything was wrong. "What's happening?"

"Pain. I can't stay."

I told Marilyn. She and Rog scurried to make dinner. We ate and posed for final photos. We started for home—a five-hour drive. As soon as were in the car, Marv fell over on my lap in the back seat and slept. About two hours in, he awakened long enough to join us for double-scoop ice cream cones (we'd spotted a place on the way up). As soon as we started again, Marv was asleep, his head on my lap. Later, in the darkness, I finagled my phone out of my purse and took a photo of my warm hand over his. His watch read 9:40 p.m.

To me, this was a huge change. This was not my husband. I could not recall that he'd ever fallen over onto my lap and fallen asleep. We arrived home at one this morning, so thankful Jon and Sheri had flown home to make Marv's last wish happen—to go back "home" for a final time on the Fourth of July.

CHAPTER EIGHTEEN

Monday, July 9, 2018

Email

To: Family and Friends

From: Marv

1. My health update: I am continuing to be quite healthy, although experiencing some difficulty sleeping. However, I seem to be rather hyper and my thinking is running full steam ahead. I have good energy, and my mind is very "good."

2. We have decided to hold on our trip to Chicago until later this month. I will keep you updated on its status and my health condition. Currently, I no longer am driving, so Lois has the task. We planned to drive to Chicago and would visit a few days to see some folks for the final time.

3. Fourth of July trip to Prinsburg, Minnesota. This was a fun trip and I enjoyed seeing about 50 former classmates from high school years. Weather, except for a brief shower in the morning, was great although humid. Enjoyed the parade in the late afternoon and spending time with family, cousins, and others. On the evening of the Fourth, we went

to Willmar for our hotel and then drove on to Rog and Marilyn's lakefront home for the day. We drove home in the evening, five hours from Minneapolis, arriving home about 1:15 a.m. I had not slept well on the Fourth so was glad to return home for a good night's rest. Loved Rog and Marilyn's hospitality and the pontoon ride on the lake.

4. I'm continuing to do some writing and consultation for my business, TAMES/HRS, and hope to propose some additional federal legislation for this fall. It will depend on the results of the election in November.

5. I'm very interested in having a conversation with a few of you concerning my book. I'm most interested in your reaction to it and some of the things I tried to accomplish. It has been quite a journey that I have felt very good about. Lois and I have had a tremendous time together since January's diagnosis.

6. Plans still pending are to have dinners and lunches with each of you. No decision on where we will be staying. More later.

7. Love you all and appreciate your thoughts and prayers.

Marv

Words from Marv

I think we have to be willing to take somebody in and help them. We need to find ways to help people, regardless of their unique and challenging circumstances.

When I was developing programs for children with disabilities, I looked for ways to meet the specific needs of different kids. I looked for ways to change the system for the better, for ways to get kids out of their homes and help them. We had a young girl with cerebral palsy, years ago. She was probably extremely bright, like other CP kids, but she couldn't communicate. In the 1970s we made a communication board for her—the first communication board. There were pictures she could point at that were used to communicate. Nowadays, people have computers that help them do that far better. Stephen Hawking had one and was able to communicate because of it. We should never limit kids because of their disabilities. We need to give them a chance.

I don't like it when people tell me I can't do something, so I took my idea and started to run with it.

When I started TAMES/HRS, I took little pay the first couple of years. I wanted to make sure my employees were paid every two weeks and the monthly federal tax deposits were made. This put a strain on our home family budget! I joked with Lois that she was at least able to go to bed with me. She didn't think that was a good enough pay-out, though.

The company continued to grow from 1996 to 2016. I hired additional staff, including a series of executive directors who did not work out. When interviewing candidates, I liked to use a question I had used when doing this task with SMA. "What's the correct way to hold a spatula?" The candidate's answer would indicate to me how flexible they might be or if they were likely to be rigid.

The correct answer is, "Whatever way it works." The usual answer, while looking at their hand, would be to use one's right or left hand. But what does one do if you have no hands?

I learned this from knowing a lady who was born with no hands. She used her feet like they were hands—shopping for fruit, groceries, and even writing out checks. She was amazing.

Since we were dealing with children with disabilities and creating a new billing service, I wanted people who would be creative; however, they are hard to find. That question became a part of my reputation.

Notes

When I forwarded Marv's bulleted note from today to his siblings, I did not have the heart to tell him there would be no more trips. No more dinners. No more lunches. None. No way could I plan all those stops and hotels again and do all the driving and be ready to care for him in his present unstable condition.

CHAPTER NINETEEN

Tuesday, July 10, 2018

Email

To: Kids

Dad had his second sleepless night. I gave him extra meds last night hoping they would help, but he was up at three. He'd wanted to go to Menards and Kath's today, but he went back to bed, for the third time, at ten, hoping to sleep. Last night in our bedtime prayer, he acknowledged, for the first time, that things were getting difficult.

I don't know what if anything this means, but the books say change in night/day patterns and excessive sleepiness (falling asleep in chair mid-conversation) could herald the final days/weeks. He's also had frontal headaches. So far he's taking his own aspirin for those, and it is helping. He's had no shortness of breath.

Otherwise, we're working to control his muscle cramping in legs and hands and abdominal distension, some of which is due to elimination problems. I have several meds I can give as I see fit. Dad is very agreeable and takes whatever I suggest.

Our most recent hospice visit was Friday. We anticipate one tomorrow again. Dad sees no need to have one earlier.

This morning, he outlined what he still wanted to do for me. It involves financial projections for 2019 and 2020. He said, chuckling a bit, he wants me to be able to live until 95 without having to go on food stamps. I have some of this info already, but apparently there's more he wants to have for me concerning stuff like projected dividends.

We are looking forward to out-of-town friends coming at one. They are near us at Good Earth State Park at a family reunion. Our pastor was going to come at one, but I have him on standby for when Dad is awake and alert. If Dad needs a nap while our company is here, I'll offer to take them to see Falls Park downtown.

We have our Reserve [HOA] monthly dinner at our clubhouse tonight. Not sure we'll make it, but I can run up and get plates of food to bring home.

So it's quiet here with only the washer and dryer going. I purged my closet yesterday. Am washing around forty items to donate to our church's garage sale later in July. Dad wants to donate most of his clothes too.

Have a good day, all. It's fun to see Kathleen's photos of Madison and Jacob riding the waves at South Haven. Kyle and Kaileen are coming at one tomorrow to pick up the coffee table Dad made— the legs finally worked out. And Dad's got Kath's old outdoor bench packed up in the Forester for delivery. He told our neighbor that Jon did a great job cutting the new boards, which they got from a construction site dumpster, for the seat. Dad wants to paint the bench at Kath's once she decides on the color.

Dad is now up and says he slept well (45 minutes). "Popcorn naps," I used to call them— now he's down, now he's up. Time for a suppository. Dad loves that I'm in charge of his bowels. Ha. We still have lots of humor, even though he told me this morning he's not been a very good (i.e., awake) companion for me the last few days. Now, I must take care of the washing and cajole him out of his frayed cutoff jeans and stained orange T-shirt to be ready for company.

Email

To: Marianna

Days seem to go so fast. TID [three times a day] and PRN [whenever necessary] meds. Went to get groceries yesterday for the first time in our marriage while Marv slept. He'd made the list.

A nurse cousin we saw in Prinsburg thinks Marv's liver is enlarged. I've never been good at assessing livers, but his stomach is so distended and hard and percusses dull on that side, as opposed to the tympani on the other gassy side.

Now, he's at his computer as if it's another normal day. Roller coaster.

Must get myself ready for guests. Marv's had his suppository and changed his clothes. Yay!

Thursday, July 12, 2018

Email

To: Kids and My Sisters

A poor day. Marv up every hour all last night. Did not call me. Now it's nine o'clock. He's worn out. To bed. Slept only two forty-five-minute naps all day. Abdomen remains brick-hard and painful. Has some gurgling sounds, which is hopeful. Headache and cramps in calves, arms, and hands continue. We are happy we are at home and not in Chicago as Marv wished for this week. There's no place like home in our own bed. He said, with a smile, "If I'm not here in the morning, it's been nice." I replied, grinning, "It's been a blast. You are so lucky. Not every husband gets his wife checking him for fecal impaction." He shrugged me off as if to acknowledge that since he wants to remain at home, he has no choice. Humor remains.

He reported some instances of double vision today. Meds? Brain tumor?

Friday, July 13, 2018

Notes

Marv slept till five. Very groggy. His leg shaking woke me up, and I found him on the edge of the bed. I barely got him to the bathroom because he was so unsteady. Got him back to my side of the bed. He knew enough to shimmy to his side.

I twisted the hem of his T-shirt around my hand so I would know if he tried to get up. I woke up at eight thirty. Yay!

Nurse here. Due to no response from all interventions last night, we decided he should go inpatient for further assessment.

Got to hospice facility at eleven thirty. Marv still unsteady. Nurse came in. No doctor. Computer down, so they can't get Marv's record up now. He told her he was only going to stay four hours (semi-jokingly), so she'd better do what she had to do. He needed a cigarette, so we lurched out to car, me hanging on. Lunch came. He sat on edge of bed and dug in. He did not offer me anything, very unlike him. Normally he'd know I'd be hungry too. I took (or snuck) two bites of everything on his tray—fish, beets, mashed potatoes, blueberry bread, and vegetable soup, and one bite of coconut cream pie—just enough calories to keep me going for a while. An aide brought in three cookies; two were chocolate chip. Marv said I could have them. Luckily for still-hungry me, he doesn't like chocolate chips.

Marv kept asking anyone who walked in, or walked by, when he would see a doctor. They all said they'd ask. Finally, at one thirty, he fell asleep. I collapsed into the one easy chair in the room, leaned back, and took a photo of him, tears spewing helter-skelter down my face. He was *finally* resting, and I could let my pretenses drop. Oh, he had been so anxious otherwise; his restless body language said he was ready to torpedo out of there.

He'd just awakened when a nurse came in and said the doctor on call had ordered Miralax times four every three hours.

Marv asked, "Lois can give that to me at home, right? I want to leave. Now. My four hours are up."

The nurse was terrific! She executed the discharge order pronto, and we were on our way home.

Once we got home, after a cigarette outside, Marv fell into bed and was out. I was so exhausted, but my nerves were too tight to relax. I tried to lie down on the couch but sprang up like I had to go somewhere or do something. I checked on Marv; he was sound asleep. I grabbed my purse, jumped into my Beetle, and raced to my Starbucks a mile away. Got my favorite—a decaf grande mocha frappuccino, iced. Thought I owed it to myself. Had to chuckle a bit, as during my weekly conversations with the hospice chaplain, she'd been telling me to take care of myself. I'd have to report that I was trying.

Email

To: Kids and My Sisters

Dad up from one-hour nap at five in the afternoon. Thought it was five in the morning and wondered why I wasn't in bed but was all dressed folding sheets from the dryer. He'd been to Palos Heights [a former home] in his dream and was walking in our old backyard in his underwear finding woodchucks. He thinks what would cure his problems is a good screwing with me! Instead, he's sitting inside the open side door of the garage in his underwear having a cigarette. I hope he doesn't wander down the street. Ha. He is planning on Raisin Bran for dinner. I think I mentioned that he now clearly sees two fire hydrants across the street where there is one, and he sees two large wheel/fans on the one wheel of his John Deere planter. This is probably due to the brain tumor. Our social worker showed up as we were negotiating leaving the hospice house. She asked if he saw two of her. He laughed. "Handling one of you is enough." She is young and has a good rapport with him. She was able to help assure the inpatient staff that this guy is serious about dying at home.

Thanks for being there for me! I've decided my consultant/caretaking services are worth $200/hour; I'll be deducting that from your inheritance. Dad agrees I'm priceless, especially when I'm doing what I need to do to deal with his elimination problems. The hospice nurse affirmed my worth to him, and he agreed to that too.

Time to get our Raisin Bran dinner. Maybe I can fancy it up with Cool Whip.

Saturday, July 14, 2018

Notes

Marv up and down all night. Gave laxatives times three.

5:50 a.m. In extreme pain. 9/10. Woke me up. He said, "Time to go to ER." I called hospice and said, "I know ER won't be the answer. I just need to calm him." She gave instructions for three medications every half hour until comfortable. The goal is to "snow (sedate) him," calm him down, relieve the pain. She also changed dosages and times on nine other meds. Marv very agreeable to the plan.

While the meds took hold, I lay on the bed with him. We stared into each other's eyes. The pain and fear were almost more than I could bear. I assured him, "Honey, I'll be here. These meds will work." He closed his eyes and drifted off.

At 9:40, I woke him up for his nine o'clock meds. He was alert, oriented. Pain 1.5/10. He got dressed. Was intermittently steady on his feet. He stood by the bar and cut his pads in half. (He's worn incontinence pads since his prostate cancer surgery in 1999; he always cut his pads in half because "I only use a half, so why waste the other half?") He went outside to smoke.

A Yellow Cab delivered the latest med changes. The regular Avera delivery guys must not work weekends.

Marv was slicing a pork roast at the bar. He had to stop a minute while I gave him a shot. "Hurry up, honey. I'm busy." Later that morning, he watered the flowers on the berm in the backyard. He nearly tripped on the hose.

At noon, he came in. Said his balance feels off. Feels like he can sleep. Says his abdominal pain is returning, a "good 2/10." Wants to go to bed. I gave him all his meds. He asked if I'd contacted Jeremy (the publisher who did his book). He'd asked that I contact him to videotape him giving the children's sermon where he releases a balloon to show the kids where souls go after death. I told him I wanted to read his book again to check all my edits before I contacted Jeremy.

I felt bad; that was a bit of a lie. I didn't see him as able to pull off a children's sermon anymore. He wants to go to Kath's tomorrow and water her flowers one more time before they come home from vacation. Not sure if that will happen either.

Nurse here at four. Got orders from hospice doctor for different laxatives. She went out to buy them. I was busy giving Marv meds all evening. Finally, at 10:00, he passed "chocolate pudding." Anytime he passes anything, I'm elated. States no pain at present. I gave him bedtime meds at eleven.

Sunday, July 15, 2018

Notes

Marv was up several times during the night. Groggy. Unsteady. Hospice called at nine this morning. The plan now is to medicate for "agitation/terminal restlessness." Marv in and out, smoking. He made out a Menards list. I texted Kath. They just passed Madison, Wisconsin, on their way home. I asked her to call Marv and ask questions. I jotted down Marv's responses: "Feeling pretty good. Not sleeping through the night. No solid stool. Stomach hard. If you see water coming out of my ears, you'll know how much I've been drinking. A little balance issue."

I gave him the morning meds, told him there'll be no Menards today. He asked, "Why not?" I said, "The nurse said." He said, "That's two against one." I said, "The doctor told the nurse, so that's three against one."

Up for coffee and cigarette and down for short naps all day. Asked for newspaper, Bold Coffee, and a Heath bar from the gas station. I drove up to get them. He dropped his coffee twice and smudged the Heath bar on his jean shorts and T-shirt.

At 2:45 p.m., he was sitting outside. "I want to go to Perkins tonight for scrambled eggs." I told him it was time to nap first. We could go to Perkins when Kath got home. He needed my heavy assistance to get back into the house and into bed. As I hung on to him while walking, I tried to reassure him with, "Honey, you have only a little time left." He mumbled groggily, "We'll see." What a surreal conversation.

At five, hospice called. I asked, "How long will this go on?" She said up to three days after he stops eating. She said Marv should not smoke anymore. Not sure how that's going to go over.

Kath and family came. Marv up, insisting on going to Perkins. We said we'd go. I told him the nurse said no more smoking. I don't even remember why, other than since he'd dropped his hot coffee he wasn't safe with lighters anymore. His face and voice got very firm. "I can move out, you know. Get my own apartment." I gave him calming meds. We went to Perkins.

At Perkins, he said he wanted pancakes. Then his eyes glazed over, and he stared into space. When Kath's food came first, he was sitting next to her and reached for her plate. She told him it was hers. He did the same thing with my plate. When his food came, he ate two eggs, bacon, and hash browns. Never touched his pancakes but put syrup on his hash browns.

On a photo taken of us at the table, Marv looks dazed, looking off to the side, as if not paying attention.

When we stood to leave, he had to go to the bathroom. He headed toward the kitchen. I assisted him, and we got him home.

A hospice nurse called at eight. Gave me detailed instructions of medication dosages and frequencies. Said she was on call from ten until eight the next morning. I should call anytime.

I was enormously comforted by all the nurses. Even as a nurse myself, I could not see my situation clearly. My fatigue was too great. Nonetheless, I would fulfill my promise to Marv. I would make sure he would die at home the way he wished.

That had been easy to say all along, but we never could have known how things would go toward the end. I did not anticipate his losing the ability to reason. I didn't even think about how I'd be after losing a few nights' sleep, even though I know very well that I must have sleep to function. And I'd been on my own for the past week with my daughter and family on vacation and our son and wife back at their West Coast home.

Monday, July 16, 2018

Notes

Early this morning, I heard Marv get up at four and then heard nothing until 6:20. In a thick fog of sleep, I caught a faint pinging sound coming through the laundry room from the garage. I plopped my hand on Marv's side of the bed—empty. I zipped out of bed to the garage. Discovered Marv belted into the Forester, wearing khaki shorts with an undershirt. Opened door. His eyes were wild, vacant, staring. Eerie.

"Where are you going?" I asked softly while my heart thumped with fear.

"To the station. But the car won't start. Did you take my keys?"

I quickly figured out he wanted his cigarettes. I'd hidden them and his keys after the nurse had impressed upon me he wasn't safe anymore. "I have your cigarettes, honey. Come. I'll get them for you."

When he got out of the car, I noticed he was wearing only one tennis shoe. He sat outside with his coffee and cigarettes. Told me he couldn't find his other shoe.

I collapsed into a lawn chair next to him. My body shook and shuddered. I took deep breaths, in and out. What if I'd not hidden the keys? What if I'd not heard that tiny ping when he'd pushed the ignition? What if he'd been able to start the car? My mind couldn't go there. Not only for his safety but everyone's out on the road. I was so worried and so tired, I couldn't even cry.

Hospice called at eight thirty. She came, stayed an hour. She must have seen I was a wreck. She suggested door magnets that ping when doors are opened. All I could think of was the leather wrist and ankle restraints I had used on patients years before. She also said to put all medications out of sight during the night. I had to find a place for the arsenal we'd collected. They now covered half the kitchen table.

Marv assumed a routine of up and down every half hour or so. Midafternoon, he decided he wanted to go to Hy-Vee, his favorite grocery store. He worked on a list. When we got home, I wrote these notes:

1. Left his list at home. I saw it and took it along. When in store, he dropped the list three times.

2. He hung on to me in the parking lot; he knew he was unsteady.

3. He got turned around in the store. Insisted we had to turn down a left aisle to get milk. I said, "I think we go straight." He barked, "And who does the shopping for us?" I followed him where he wanted to go. We landed back at the entrance. He said, "They must have rearranged everything. I'll have to get used to it."

4. I asked him to get green peppers and directed him to the produce section. When I caught up with him, he had peaches.

5. He kept saying we needed sausages; we had plenty.

6. He insisted on pushing the cart and bumped into displays and people.

7. He squinted when trying to read the overhead signage as if he couldn't make out the words.

8. He could not locate the Hy-Vee card in his billfold. He gave me his credit card to pay.

9. We went to the store for five items and wound up spending $80.

It was clear nothing was making sense to him, and certainly his behavior was way out of whack for me. As I wrote those notes, I felt dissociated, like I was once again documenting the behavior of a patient. It was my way of coping, I think. I could not believe this was Marv, the husband I'd relied on for so long.

I paused and pulled up some fun stuff from my memories: our long and quiet chats after dinner; our sharing a study and him issuing requests and me answering I wasn't his secretary; our long-standing joke that I must not ask him to help me with computer problems. With the latter, he'd grin as if I'd never understand and ask in a teasing voice, "Don't you know that could cause a divorce?"

Returning to my notes, I felt disloyal writing all the "failures" down. But Marv had said, "Keep track, honey, of this time. Whatever we go through may help someone else someday. When you write your book."

That evening, there were more mishaps. While he was fussing with the TV remote, the channel changed. "What did you do now?" he barked. I'd done nothing, so I asked what channel he wanted to watch. He couldn't say. I ventured, "607, 611, 614?" "No, no, no." I asked, "CNN?" "Yes," he said, with an exasperated sigh.

There was a bright spot. He figured out how to return a call to a cousin. From what I overheard, he had a lucid conversation with her. When he hung up, he was almost his normal self. He had a relaxed face. There was some weaving a bit in his gait, but he got himself to bed, slowly. However, in our nightly prayers, he left out the names of our kids and grandkids—the first time he'd forgotten since he received his diagnosis in Dodge City nearly six months earlier. Before he fell asleep, he said he wanted to be more awake tomorrow so he could work at Kath's house. His fingers fidgeted with the sheets until he drifted off. His tummy was a bit softer but still large.

Blog Post

Catch up time! It's been a while since I blogged.

If I had a penny for all the good things that have happened since Marv's cancer—for all the heartfelt hugs I've seen him give his siblings, family, and friends, and for all the sacrifices our children have made to take care of us older folks—the pennies would easily overflow an old metal milk can Marv has talked about from his childhood days on the farm.

We are now facing reality. Hospice remains our lifeline. Last week friends from Chicago spent three hours with us, a huge gift as they broke away from other obligations in our area. Our pastor came for another two-hour visit. New friends came for coffee. And neighbors stop by to talk to Marv as he sits out front on a lawn chair.

Yesterday morning, we missed church for the first time; I'm hoping we'll be able to go again soon.

And now we are off to another week. Thank you, everyone, for all your prayers and encouragement.

In Retrospect

Mulling over that time of change in Marv's condition, I realize I needed the prior weeks to prepare for his death. I can't imagine how people can handle the sudden or quick deaths of their loved ones. I'm grateful we had the time to do the paperwork—and the emotional work—to get ready to let go. As a nurse, I realized too that I needed to be Marv's caregiver. I needed to be a part of the process, to see every step firsthand. I needed control, to know everything was done right.

PART V

ENTERING THE VALLEY

CHAPTER TWENTY

Tuesday July 17, 2018

In Retrospect

I didn't know when I started my notes for this week that it would be Marv's last. It was as if he had fulfilled his final wish of going to Prinsburg, and he was now ready to die. A hospice brochure had told me what to look for, yet I still wasn't ready. The overall change seemed to creep in, but the demand for twenty-four-hour surveillance stormed in overnight. I found myself going through caregiving motions in robotic fashion, with no time to process.

I continued my charting, including recording details about the persistent and painful elimination problem. These details would become vital in reporting to our hospice nurses, and I hope they will be valuable to my readers as well.

Notes

On Tuesday, the 17th, my day started early.

4:30 a.m.   Awake. Marv dressed self slowly. Took morphine for complaints of abdominal pain. Took Haldol for antsy-ness.

Groggy. Very unsteady. I guided him into the kitchen, his body felt rigid, as if on automatic, to get cigarette and coffee.

Both sat, mostly silent, inside garage by side door until six, then back to bed.

8:00   Up again. Dressed self. Teetered but could walk alone. I could not get up, way too tired. He had "escaped" my belt pinned to his side of the bed and looped on my wrist. I had to trust he'd be okay.

9:00   I woke up. Marv asleep on couch. Complaining of abdominal pain. Sitting outside with me. Quiet. Explains his teetering walk as "getting older." Said he had a Pop Tart for breakfast, but an opened packet, still full, is on the counter.

Burping often. Says he's not passed gas. Says he's so sleepy. (Six hours since morphine and Haldol.) Says, with chuckle, "You're devious when you ask me how many fire hydrants I'm seeing." Answered, "One!" (He'd been seeing two where there was one.)

11:00   Marv at computer. Looks dazed. Staring at the screen as if a foreign object. Marv trying to call our HOA about our sprinkler. Got angry with me for telling him his phone was ringing when he was saying "Hello, hello" to the ringing phone. Told him he could call them later, to take a nap now, I'd call him in an hour.

On the way to bed, he forcefully told me to leave him alone. Called me a dingbat, something he had never done and would never do. Had to remind myself his brain is not working normally, he's extremely uncomfortable, so I can't take this personally. As he fell on the bed, I reminded him, in a silly joke between us, that I'd try to learn but "you know I've always been a slow learner." He'd already drifted off.

11:30   I called my sister, crying, and then cried/sobbed for fifteen minutes. It is so hard seeing Marv like this; our relationship feels annihilated overnight. Called our neighbor to notify our HOA about sprinkler problem so I can tell Marv she's handling it.

12:00pm   I called Marianna. Cried more. Talked about whether I'll be able to care for Marv at home until the end. I'm so very tired. I should be able to answer that soon.

12:20   Our new mirrors and light fixtures arrived for the master bath.

2:30   Kyle and Kaileen here for an hour. They vacuumed carpeting and washed our tile floors. I took photo of them and Marv with the finished coffee table. Marv had finally figured out how to cut the legs. His abdomen looks about the size of a six-month pregnancy.

3:30   Kath got an appointment to have regrowth of Marv's nodule on right side removed on July 30. Marv insisting it be removed, I think because it's visible evidence of the cancer. She got number for Comfort Keepers. I set up appointment for Monday (7/23) at three, the earliest they can come. I absolutely need help so I can sleep.

4:00   We both rested. I feel as though I should never sleep; I should be vigilant every minute.

5:00   Marv tried to make dinner. Needed help. He couldn't find the chip dip in fridge. Was right where it usually is. Ate chip dip off my plate while waiting for microwave. His plate had chips and dip and a sweet roll (that I never have; normally, he would have known he was eating off the wrong plate).

8:00   Marv increasingly irritable. Wants no more pills or liquids. Resists explanations for why he should take them. Says, "You listen too much to the doctors and nurses and should stop." Says he may leave. Insisting *Wheel of Fortune* is on Channel 2. When I turned it to Channel 7, he ordered me to turn it back. When he saw *Entertainment Tonight*, he said, "Turn it back to 7."

9:30   Says he's tired enough to go to bed. I run with whatever he says.

10:00   Showered. In bed. Me too. Asked me if the ceiling was falling down and hanging below the ceiling fan. Said I had pine cones on my shoulder that "didn't win." Said I was pulling faces at him (I wasn't looking at him). Said men were trying to take something off our headboard. Said I had burberries on my forehead. I asked, "What kind of berries?" He spelled out slowly and loudly, "B I R T H D A Y. Birthday."

10:45   I called hospice nurse to report new hallucinations, even after all the med changes. She gave me new instructions: "Goal now is to medicate him and save him from that discomfort." I had to digest her rationale: save him from the discomfort of his hallucinations. Hadn't thought of that. I wasn't ready to snow him into oblivion yet, but this rationale made sense. Gave him the new meds.

11:30   Awake and mumbling. I helped him up to the bathroom. Then he finally slept.

Email

To: All Family

From: Kathleen

Another restless night for Dad (and in turn, Mom). Both were up 4:30 to 6:00 a.m. Then back to bed. Mom woke up around 9:30 to find Dad fully dressed on the couch. He said he got up at 8:30. Front door was open, his chair outside. Mom had her bathrobe belt pinned to the bottom sheet on his side of the bed and had wrapped it around him and wrapped the other end around her hand. He still managed to escape. Mom is completely spent. Lots of tears. Overtired. He's not the man she knows him to be and not the person he would want to be. Dad is oblivious to his up/down/all-around routine. Continues to think he can mow my lawn, do his own errands, etc. He is not consistently steady on his feet and is unable to focus and/or make eye contact like he used to. Very sad. He looks so lost.

Mom reached out to Comfort Keepers. Meeting set up for next Monday. They offer CNA services that would help provide Mom a much-needed break—especially if sleeping patterns continue to be erratic.

Mom in desperate need of sleep. At ten last night, Mom had Dad medicated and in bed. He showered (which he needed to do—started looking a tad "ripe"). She prayed with him and asked God to help her (and him) get this through this. Dad apologized for being short with her and said to "hang in" and gave her several kisses on her forehead. He then started hallucinating again, seeing "birthday berries" on her cheeks.

Mom called the hospice nurse, who gave Mom an order for a "medication cocktail" to try to reduce Dad's hallucinations and promote sleep. Nurse provided Mom with reassurance and much-needed comfort. Mom really likes the nurses. They have been a tremendous lifeline for her.

Interlude . . .

The Lord is my shepherd; I shall not want.

He maketh me to lie down in green pastures: he leadeth me beside still waters.

He restoreth my soul: he leadeth me in the paths of righteousness for his name's sake.

Yea, though I walk through the valley of the shadow of death, I will fear no evil: for thou art with me; thy rod and thy staff they comfort me.

Thou preparest a table before me in the presence of mine enemies: thou anointest my head with oil; my cup runneth over.

Surely goodness and mercy shall follow me all the days of my life: and I will dwell in the house of the Lord forever.

—Psalm 23

Wednesday, July 18, 2018

Notes

Marv was up at six thirty. I heard him first in the bathroom. I'd put Santa bells on the bedroom door out to the hallway, and I heard those when he left the room. At least that system for alerting me is working for now. He said he slept all night, but my note telling him to call me if he wanted a cigarette was gone. When I asked, he said he'd put it in the wastebasket. (I didn't find it.) And the fleece throw was rearranged on the couch. When I reported that to the nurse, she asked with a chuckle, "Are you maybe hallucinating now?" The nurses are terrific, helping me stay sane.

Marv made his own breakfast—fried egg, bread with honey, microwaved sausage. Ate outside on his usual chair. He napped and passed a few teeny stools (yay!). Then he was up until around nine thirty. Complained of slight headache, leg aches, and tight belly. Mind is clearer tonight. Worked at his computer awhile and was a tad more conversant. He likes when neighbors come up the driveway to talk when he's sitting outside with his coffee and cigarette.

At eleven, he was up to the bathroom. Passed a few more teeny-formed stools. Passing gas. I tried to reassure him these are all good signs. Some of the new meds may be working.

Email

To: All Family

From: Kathleen

I dropped my kids off at school and went over to Mom and Dad's. Arrived around nine. Both were up. It was a better night, but not a full, restful night. Dad continues his confusion. He is insistent that he would like a nodule removed from his right side (where cancer was removed before). Said, "It's filled with cancer, it needs to be removed." Mom said, "Your brain has cancer." Dad said, "Well, you can't remove that." LOL! Dad wanted to go to Staples for printer cartridges and paper. When we got there, he grabbed a pack of paper. Then he went to get cartridges. He didn't have right printer info. Insisted on a certain one, and it wasn't correct. He then said he needed to use the bathroom.

Mom helped him to the bathroom. I stood outside holding the printer paper. When he came out of the bathroom, I said, "Shall we go buy this paper?" He said, "No, we don't need paper."

I then asked, "Where would you like to go for lunch?" His response: "Staples."

We went to Culver's. He wolfed down a hamburger, onion rings, and cheese curds. Sheesh! I asked Dad if there was anything else he needed to do. He said, "No, I am checking out." We went home, and he took a nap.

Dad had several "turds" today—his words. I started laughing as he was telling the nurse about his turds. No one uses that word. He also burps at random and makes no bones about how loud he is. If we don't laugh, we would just keep on crying.

Sara offered a wonderful listening ear. She said she also noticed a considerable difference in Dad from over a week ago, before her vacation. Lack of eye contact, lack of engagement in conversation, unsteady gait, and overall blank stare.

I am pooped (pun intended). Need to get some rest to gear up for my shift tomorrow.

Thursday, July 19, 2018

Email

To: Chicago Nursing Friends [two friends who walked alongside me during Marv's illness]

To you nurses only: you may share generalities with others. Our daughter has taken the reins since returning from her vacation last Sunday. It takes a village. . . .

I'm trying to keep Marv home because at the hospice house he'd be medicated into oblivion and given a nicotine patch. But he has lost the capacity for "insight," so there's no reasoning with him. He rarely initiates conversation anymore. Hospice suggests we have fulfilled Marv's wish for as much quality of life as possible, so it's my decision when we start medicating more. They affirm my observation and suggest his massive abdominal distension and pain and periodic hallucinations are not comfortable for him and remind me that our aim now is comfort. Decisions!

In Retrospect

Until that last month, I'd been making decisions without a problem. But as I lost more and more sleep, I no longer trusted myself and realized I needed Kathleen's help—especially with this need to medicate Marv for his comfort. Of course, we wanted to make Marv comfortable, and of course, we couldn't rely on his decision-making anymore. But it was still hard to say, "This is it. This is what I'm going to do." I know the main difficulty for me was that I never expected that I'd have to make that kind of decision alone.

We'd always made big decisions together and I never thought to ask him about this eventuality, so it felt like I'd been blindsided by something that I had not prepared for. I shuddered as I thought back to what I'd stressed to nursing students, "Always come to clinicals prepared." And now I wasn't prepared myself.

Not that I hadn't seen this happen before. A year before, I'd been with one of my sisters' two kids, the same age as mine, as they needed to make the decision about taking her off a ventilator. It had been heartbreaking to witness the nurse practitioner explain to them the horrific outcome they could expect after so many days on the ventilator if she survived. I was with them as we stood in the hallway outside her room trying to decide what she would have wanted.

Despite this, Marv and I never talked specifically about what he would want. If I'd had exact words from him saying to medicate him at the end, that would have helped. But I had to give him morphine to do that, and he had just started expressing he didn't want to take that or any meds. But it was also clear that his mind wasn't computing. I'd never seen him that way before and was having trouble comprehending that he really wasn't able to make a clear decision, even though most of the time, to all appearances, he was making perfect sense and acting normally.

It was a gut-wrenching time.

Notes

4:30 a.m.	Up several times during the night. Passing gas, teeny amounts of formed stool.
5:30	Outside with coffee and cigarette. Complaining of abdominal pain.
6:30	Back to bed. I've given him all the ordered meds, plus for anxiety.
7:45	Marv up. Later that morning, Kathleen came, thank God.

Email

To: All Family

From: Kathleen

Here's today's update on my dad (with a bit of Kathleen humor to make you laugh).

Last night was another eventful night with very limited sleep for either my mom or my dad—despite the meds cocktail that was prescribed to assist in "zonking" my dad out. He was up with cramping, gas, and bathroom needs. No hard poops yet, just diarrhea. But lots of stinky gas!

I arrived this morning with Mom's requested order—enema bag and tubing, and four packs of Virginia Slims—only to see my mom looking near death herself. My dad was out having a smoke, none the wiser. He told me that he slept fine and that Mom would too, if she didn't "hide" everything from him and thereby make him have to ask her where things are (cigarettes being the main thing). He lit up a cigarette in the house the other day—something he hasn't done ever. He knows that smoking is not allowed in the house.

So I sent Mom for her 10:00 a.m. massage and gave her my garage door opener. Told her to go to my place after her massage and get some uninterrupted sleep. In other words: Don't come back—I've got Dad covered.

Notes

10:00 a.m.	Had my massage and went to Kath's to sleep. So important, so helpful. Was out, out, out for several hours. My body is beyond weary. Then went home.
1:00–3:30 p.m.	Marv napped. Then up. Routine now is a few minutes at the computer, back and forth outside with coffee and cigarettes, opening mail, watching news, interspersed with dozing. Kath and I sit together with him or separately. He made eggs for our supper and had a small glass of Riesling "for my nerves."
7ish	Nurse Sara called: "Keep him as comfortable as possible."
8:30	Marv had sudden outburst when I went to give him his evening meds. He wants "no more meds—they don't work anyway." Taking the meds from me, he said, "These are the last ones I'll take." I quietly say, "I know, honey."
10:30	Showered. In bed. He insisted on no more pills. I said, "Just a few little ones yet." He said, "Sheesh. Enough." I gave him three meds for sleep and anxiety.

He does not want to be snowed: "I still have things to do." He wants no help at the computer; I see his blank stares at the computer and piles of scribbled notes, and I've sat down next to him and offered help, but he waves me away.

That night he prayed, "God help us through this valley of the shadow of death." I asked, "Honey, how I can make this easier?" He smiled wanly and whispered, "You just need to be controlled."

I caught his humor. We've never "taken orders" from each other. He's always told me that's why he loves me—I'm independent. Whenever he's told me something to do, he's always added, "That's just a suggestion," because he knows I'm not likely to do as he says or at least he wants me to have the freedom to do what I decide. And now, here we are in a position of me having to give him medication against his will for a benefit he can't see and a need he can't understand. I have to remind myself to breathe; my chest feels as though it's tightly wrapped in a cloth restraint.

Friday, July 20, 2018

Notes

12:00 a.m.   Marv up with horrendous pain. Bent over sink groaning. Passed teeny amount of gas. Burping. No relief. Tummy so hard! Agreed to take four meds for the acute pain. Back to bed. Groaning. Groaning. Groaning. My eyes swelled with tears: tears of feeling helpless to make things better for him, tears of sleeplessness. Can't imagine how he is bearing this pain with such little sound. His voice never rises, just periodic guttural exhalations of deep pain.

8:30   Still sleeping. Last up with my help at 3:00 for bathroom.

11:00   Nurse Sara is here. And social worker Kelly. Marv
               awake briefly. When they asked what he saw as an
               alternative to taking pain meds, he said, "I'm ready
               to go. Or pass." That was not a term he'd used. Did
               he for sure mean "die"?

               Later, I needed Kath to help me get him to the
               bathroom. We rolled him back to bed on his office
               chair.

He was up and down the rest of day, sometimes steadier than others. He read his emails on his tablet outside. Out of the blue, he said, "Tomorrow will be my last." I asked, "The last of what?" "The last of my passage."

I wanted to ask more. Was his "passage" this experience? I felt so dense. I wanted to hang on to him and talk and talk and talk. It wasn't his style to perseverate like me, but I knew also that it was already too late to pump him for information. It felt way too intrusive. I wondered why I hadn't pumped him earlier, and I recalled I'd tried once or twice. Even recently I'd tried, asking, "Have you ever regretted not taking chemo?" He'd answered firmly, "No." End of talk.

He's planning to tell hospice tomorrow that he wants to go off all his meds and only take his Tylenol PM. "That has always worked for me." I could not get him to understand the Tylenol had worked for him when he didn't have cancer. Having cancer is a way different kind of pain.

At midnight, I told him it was time to come inside. He wanted to stay outside. I told him we all needed to rest (Kathleen was here). I got him to come inside and take four sleep and pain meds. I hoped he'd be able to sleep.

CHAPTER TWENTY-ONE

Saturday, July 21, 2018

Notes

My hope that Marv would be able to sleep did not pan out. I was barely asleep when I heard him stir.

2:00–5:00 a.m.	We were up. Outside with coffee and cigarettes. Sitting quietly. Marv staring off into distance. Eerily silent. Warm. Slight breeze. I wanted to ask what he was thinking, but it felt like he'd said all he needed to say. I'd stroke his hand, and now and then we'd lock eyes. I could not comprehend that this was how our life together was going to end. The last few days have seemed so strange. After all, he'd done so well for much longer than predicted. I guess I'd simply thought that would continue.
3:00	Marv made oatmeal with my standby assistance. Kathleen had decided to stay and got up to join us from four to five. She was surprised she'd not heard us up all night. We all went back to bed until six.

6:00   Marv up and showered. Wanted his Tylenol PM.
                    I gave him plain Tylenol so he could stay awake,
                    which he wanted to do, and also talked him into
                    taking an anti-anxiety med. He didn't want it.
                    I convinced him, with his poor night, he'd feel
                    better. He stood out front with a hose and watered
                    the brightly blooming red and yellow flowers he'd
                    planted between the green perennials skirting the
                    house. I took a video. Nothing looked awry. It
                    could have been his normal activity for a morning.

When he came back in, he said, "I'm going to tell hospice today I'm
going to quit everything. They haven't done a thing." Thankfully,
Kathleen took him for a massage, and I could rest.

Hospice came at one o'clock. The nurse who came had only
been here once. We were sitting outside when she arrived. I'd pulled
up another lawn chair for her. She'd barely introduced herself and
sat down when Marv barked, "I'm not taking any more of your
meds." His eyes popped with frustration and anger.

The nurse raised her arms as if in surrender. "You don't have
to take anything you don't want to take, Mr. Roelofs." Her quiet
demeanor exemplified caring and concern.

"Well, just know I'm done with your medications," Marv
affirmed.

She talked slowly and softly with him awhile and, miraculously
to me, got him to say that he wanted to "go through the valley of the
shadow of death with the least amount of pain." He and the nurse
agreed on a plan: he would take only what he wanted to take. But for
me, his words meant I could keep offering more than the Tylenol if
I saw stronger meds were needed to alleviate his pain.

After he finished with the nurse, Marv went into the house, ate a sandwich, and went to bed. The nurse and I talked outside and planned. To stave off hallucinations and seizures, he would have to have the meds for those, and he'd not agreed to them. But I could give them rectally. As a nurse, I knew how to do that, and since I'd been checking him rectally for stool already, I could slip in medications without him knowing. Also, as a precaution, I needed to have an injectable anti-seizure medication drawn up and ready to give immediately if he started to seize.

At two, I gave him Tylenol. At three, he requested Ibuprofen. At four, an older couple from our daughter's church came over to pray with him. They'd come once before, and I'd warned them Marv was in bed and maybe wouldn't respond much. I'd set up folding chairs on his side of the bed. When I told Marv they were here, he worked to open his eyes a bit and smiled. The gal complimented him that he had his "usual nice smile." Then she had a request—they'd had a son die when he was young, and she asked Marv to say hello to him from them in heaven. Marv loved that request. He revived for a minute or two and said in a strong voice, "I'll certainly do that. And I'll send you a postcard about the visit."

The hospice nurse called at five for a report. She said, "You have your hands full, Lois." You have no idea what the support from the nurses did for me! I was beyond tired, beyond coping in any ordinary way, but not beyond wanting desperately to be able to facilitate Marv's wish to die at home. Despite the fact he was, for real, in the process of dying, it did not feel real at all.

Marv slept most of the evening. At ten o'clock, he said, "It's time to pass." I guessed that this time, he did mean "to die." But then he refused Tylenol and Tylenol PM, saying, "I'm still here. I have stuff to do." So did he mean to die or to live longer to do more stuff? Nothing made sense to me in my state of fatigue. That night as he prayed, he thanked God for the couple's visit in the afternoon, told God about his plans to send them a postcard when he met their son, and prayed he'd be able to go to church in the morning. After he finished, I dared ask, "What are your thoughts about heaven now?" He said, "There's no pain."

We both must have drifted off, but at ten forty-five, I sensed movement on his side of the bed. I opened my eyes, adjusted my vision to the dim lighting of the nightlights, and saw him starting to slide off the edge of the bed, doubled over in pain. I grabbed for his T-shirt—clutched a hunk in my hand—and jerked myself up. I knee-walked across the bed to his side, slid down to the floor, and landed just in time to push back his knees to keep him from spilling out of bed.

I suddenly realized why he had almost fallen. My mistake. The evening before, I'd tried to think of what protective material I had in the house to put under him. I wanted to save the linens from any mishap and make it easier to clean him up in that event. I'd settled on a garbage bag and had put that under a bath towel over the bottom sheet. When he'd awakened in severe pain, he'd attempted to sit up on the edge of the bed. Of course, both he and the towel started to slide.

I fought to control tears. How could I have been so dumb? How could I think I was so smart to make up my own "blue pad" like we used in hospitals for those purposes?

Kneeling on the floor, I stabilized his legs with my hands, and he was able to shimmy himself back up on the bed. Again, in his severe pain he was making little to no sound, just deep, distant guttural groans.

I took his hands into mine, stared into his eyes, and pleaded in a whisper, "Honey, you do *not* have to suffer like this. I can give you morphine anytime you say."

I cannot describe how it felt like hours as I waited for an answer. I could feel the pulses of pain from his body attach themselves to me. It seemed we were one against the world, but only I could deliver us from this state. I reminded him again, "I can give you morphine. I promise you it will help." It was probably less than a minute later, but felt like an eternity before he whispered, "Okay."

I helped him lie down and get straight in the bed. I scurried to get the morphine. After I gave it to him, I lay next to him and lightly rubbed his brick-hard distended belly with circular motions for thirty minutes straight. A massage therapist had told me that technique once, as a good way to get things moving. Marv said it felt good and drifted away.

An hour later, at eleven forty-five, I helped him up to the bathroom. He said the edge was off his pain, but his belly was still "so tight." He went outside for coffee and a cigarette. He said he wanted to work on his computer next. Alone. I went in to lie on the couch; I hoped I would hear him come in.

Sunday, July 22, 2018

Notes

At 12:50 a.m., I asked Marv to come in from outside. He said, "I'm taking my last break. My stomach's killing me." He told me to go to bed. I asked if I could help him at the computer. He said, "No, we can go over it later this afternoon. You just go back to bed." I said, "Okay." He said, "Thanks," in a finally-you're-getting-it tone. He did not like me hovering and had made that clear several times those last few days.

At two thirty, I found him asleep on the couch.

At four thirty, I found him outside with his coffee and cigarette. I pulled up a chair. "I feel good," he announced, sounding like his usual self for the first time in days. "I passed huge amounts of gas. I can button my shorts." He showed me a two-inch gap between his tummy and belt that he said had happened at midnight. He said he was very relieved. I checked—his abdomen was still hard but a tad less taut. He agreed to take the morphine and meds that I told him "helped your tummy get this way."

We went back to bed at five. I fell sound asleep and woke up at eight thirty to find Marv dressed, sitting outside, ready to go to church. Kathleen had stayed overnight again and got up at the same time. The night before, we'd both wished he wouldn't want to go to church because we were way too drained. But there he was, so we got dressed and ready. There was no way, at that point, that we were not going to do everything he wished. Besides, he asked for so little, it was almost like we, even though dead tired, were happy to comply. Kath put incontinence supplies in her big purse in case of a mishap.

At our church, Kath's husband dropped the kids off and left to complete obligations at their own church. Kath took our photo lined up in the pew. In the photo, Marv looks handsome—short, graying hair, a bright blue, short-sleeved, button-down shirt, sprinkled with tan flowers among leaves in varying shades of green, and khaki pants. If you didn't know, you'd have to look closely to see his abdomen is struggling out against his shirt and over his belt. The telltale sign that he is not well is in his eyes. His pupils are extra-dark, staring, piercing, somewhat vacant in appearance. But I cherish that photo. Little Jacob is on his left side, Madison next to me on his right.

Marv did well in church, dozed a little. At prayer request time, I stood up. I'd not planned to, but there I was standing, looking around at the congregation in front of us.

A Sunday, early on, flashed in my mind: Marv had asked Pastor David for permission to address the congregation. He'd stood in front, looking tanned and fit, and announced, "This is what cancer looks like." He'd gone on to tell everyone he was refusing treatment. Later, I'd hear from several who'd appreciated his openness.

Now, from about the third row from the back, I started out with my voice shaking and said something like this: "You all know we were told Marv would be good for just so long and then he'd experience a significant change. That change has happened. I want to thank this church for your welcoming us so warmly these past two years and to let you know Marv is looking forward to going to his heavenly home soon."

After church, Marv told our pastor, "Have a good week." Several congregants came up to him to tell him their children had enjoyed his children's sermons. Others shook his hand.

At home, Marv sat outside with Kathleen. I was getting his meds ready when Madison asked, "May I give Grandpa his pills?" *Yes*, I thought, *he for sure would take them from her*. I followed with my camera. I wanted her to have that memory of helping relieve Grandpa's pain. The photo is adorable—she is standing, with her long blond hair, wearing an ankle-length blue floral dress, next to him with an outstretched arm, and saying, "Here's your pills, Grandpa," in her sweet, soft, nine-year-old voice. She returned to the house to play with Jacob in our playroom.

While I was sitting with Marv, he said, "Ask Madison and Jacob to come out here. Tell them Grandpa wants to talk to them." His voice was halting and sounded hoarse. There was a hint of him being short of breath, a first.

The kids came out and sat in lawn chairs across from Marv. I hovered in the garage on the other side of the open door and pressed "voice memo" on my phone. Kathleen stood near Marv. Here are excerpts of his final conversation with our youngest grandkids.

> Grandpa won't be here a week from now. When we have my funeral, I have a task for you two. [After the benediction,] you'll both go out the side door and you'll both be carrying balloons with a photo of me attached. When you go outside, you'll be releasing the balloons, so they go up into heaven saying goodbye. From then on, you'll always look up and say that's where my grandpa went. . . .
>
> I'm going to give each of you a copy of my book. When you get to be teenagers, you can read it. Keep it. That will be yours for the rest of your life. . . .
>
> So that's what will happen at my funeral. A funeral is when you celebrate someone who has passed away.

When Jacob started to slide off his seat to go play, Madison held out her arm across him: "Jacob, you gotta stay here. Grandpa's not going to be here anymore." Jake sat back in his seat, and Marv continued, "Tomorrow, I hope to come over and mow your lawn for the last time. And trim your bushes."

Madison directed a whisper toward Kath, "Is someone going to watch him?" Her mom had told the kids, due to his unsteadiness, they wouldn't be riding the tractor mower anymore with Grandpa.

Grandpa answered, his voice occasionally hesitating as he paused to think, "Your mother will be there. I'll finish that and then come home, and I've got a few more things to do for my business and for Grandma's finances. I'd like to go to Chicago yet, but that would have to be next week, but that depends totally on how I feel. .

. . I would like to see some people yet. . . . I have to have more energy. So then I'll be back tomorrow, and I'd like your mother to pick out some paint for the bench I fixed, so I can bring it back home and sand and paint it, and fix the golf cart so you can ride that down your hill and hopefully not fall over and smash your nose."

Marv's voice was giving out. Kath was fighting to hold back tears. Michael had arrived in the middle of the conversation, and he stood, expressionless, off to the side. Kath asked the kids if they had any more questions—they'd stopped Grandpa a few times talking about their neighbor who'd died, discussing their own "poop" problems when Grandpa explained his "tight, tight belly that hurts," and wondering aloud who would give them suckers after Grandpa was gone—and then she told them they could give Grandpa a hug and go in to play. Marv returned their hugs and said, "Thanks for participating in my children's sermons. They were fun."

I turned off the recorder on my phone and was thankful I'd thought to record. With a few cars passing by and me being around the corner in the garage and out of sight, I didn't get every word, but enough to catch Marv's sincerity and wish to include and to help the kids understand the process of his dying and going to heaven. To any passersby, we probably looked like we were having a normal little family chat after church on a warm, sunny, beautiful day. I don't know how we pulled it off; I know I simply did whatever had to be done.

Kathleen and family left after lunch; Marv napped. When he awakened, his pain increased over the afternoon. We continued our back-and-forth with him not wanting to take meds that weren't helping and me trying to explain that he needed at least the stronger pain med. I finally called the hospice nurse on call, who said she'd call the doctor on call to see if Marv could have a CT scan that night so we'd know what was going on. An alternative was Marv accepting the pain med and seeing about the scan tomorrow. Marv agreed to that.

Our Phoenix friends called, and Marv revved up to talk to them. He always appreciated their joshing with him that it must be hard to live with me now that I was calling the shots. He became less irritable. Kath came back and took a walk with him around the block, him saying very little.

Blog Post

A devotional came today from our former church in Chicago that feels appropriate as our family strives to be present for Marv during his final days. In it, Jesus reminds his disciples to "come away to a deserted place all by yourselves and rest awhile." I think Marv would agree we should all go away and rest awhile as he'd rather we not "hover" over him. He wants to mow our daughter's lawn, water our flowers, work at his computer, and build a cart yet, from a golf cart he retrieved from a dumpster, for our youngest grandkids to ride down a hill in their backyard.

Amidst severe pain yesterday, he informed hospice he wants to "call the shots" from now on. We're trying to keep up with his wishes.

Email

To: Marianna

I called the nurse to see if a CT scan could be done tonight. Marv is increasingly irritable and arguing that he knows his body and hospice doesn't. The nurse has been super. I cajoled Marv into morphine by syringe in his mouth, and a Phoenix friend on the phone with him agreed I should be fired for hovering. So the friend had Marv laughing while the morphine had a chance to work. The nurse offered to call her boss's boss to see if anyone was even in the CT lab tonight, and they would track down whoever could approve the cost. After I relayed all that, Marv said, docilely, "I don't want to put anyone out. I'll wait till morning."

I could have shot him.

Then he asked if I wanted to take a walk. It's blasted hot here, and I'm overheated from sitting outside with him. Just then Kath pulled up. I didn't think she was coming tonight. She is taking a walk with him.

I am lying on my couch in the A/C, venting to you. A sitcom could be made of this!

Monday, July 23, 2018

Notes

At ten last night, when Marv got ready for bed, he prayed to have his "day/night pattern fixed." He wanted to sleep all night. He accepted morphine and a few drugs of his choosing and slept peacefully until four. Then he showered. He complained of a tight, sore stomach and was rubbing it himself. He sat outside with coffee and a cigarette and watched it rain. I gave him morphine and a laxative. I reminded him he'd prayed for his nights and days to get straightened out, and God had heard. He answered, "Yeah, now we'll see how the day turns out."

At five, Marv told me, "I think I've reached the point of no return." We were sitting outside, and he was reading emails on his tablet.

At six, he complained of severe nausea and the feeling he was going to faint. I gave him morphine again because it was the only thing that would take the edge off the pain. I put in a call to hospice.

At seven, he was sleeping peacefully. I was limp with relief. It's like when you have a baby who is teething and you've done everything you know how to make them feel better to no avail, then the baby finally falls asleep, and you nearly collapse over the crib in exhaustion. Every time Marv lay down, I lay down beside him and held his hand or spooned behind him. I wondered how long I'd have his warmth—the only thing that still felt like it was him—but could not bear to dwell on the thought. In discussions about death before this cancer, he'd always told me I'd be financially taken care of, not to worry. And I'd tell him, "But a pile of dollar bills in bed won't keep me warm." Now, I thought of how we'd so lightly joked. But that was way, way before death was an active threat.

At eight, Marv woke up, swung himself into a seated position on the edge of the bed. "I have to get up. Can't sleep all day again." I wanted to say, "Just relax. Stay comfortable for now." But he was up and getting dressed before I had the words out.

At eight fifteen, he said, "I feel like something has to break loose." I asked if he'd take medication to take care of the pain and relax the abdomen. He agreed. I then asked, "What if the medication would snow you for a couple of days, or forever—that you never wake up . . .". He cut me off, "I'd be okay with that."

At last, I had his explicit okay to medicate him to the end. I took a deep breath and felt my entire body relax.

These were very somber, low-key conversations. Hesitant. A few words at a time. Like we were jointly trying to figure out how to make his final hours endurable but not admitting these were his final hours.

Email

To: My Sisters and Marianna

Marv is having a CT scan of the abdomen at four today. Pray for relief, any relief, for him. It will be good, finally, to know what is causing the enormous distension and pain and to be on a path to effective pain relief. Lots of mess to go through this morning to get far enough along to have the scan today.

Marv is so stoically handling the pain. So hard to see. Morphine barely touches. Will be able to give him more after scan is done, but I can't snow him and get him to the test at the same time. Hospice suggested again admitting him, but Marv and I agree it's much better to have him at home. As a nurse friend reminded me, I have control here; I wouldn't there. And he surely wouldn't.

Notes

We were ready at 3:30 p.m. when Kath came to take us to the hospital. Needed to help Marv up into the front seat of her Durango. Marv could not lift his legs. It was a quiet twenty-minute ride. At the hospital, I walked slowly next to Marv, ready to catch him as he swayed. I could not help but think how awfully weird it was not to be following him. With his "fast start," as our son-in-law calls Marv's usual take off, I've always walked several paces behind him. In the early days, I got annoyed with him; I wanted him to saunter with me and hold my hand. No way. If he held my hand, I'd feel pulled along as his arm naturally flexed into a rigid position, like the silly dog in toy stores at Christmas when a salesclerk would propel it on a leash, battery operated, out into the mall. Over the years, when I realized he couldn't change, I consoled myself that he had a cute butt and wasn't I lucky that I got to walk behind him.

Now, I walked beside him, one slow step at a time. We had to go to four different places—check-in, blood draw, IV start, and waiting room (where he had to drink two bottles of contrast). At each stop, Marv revived and greeted folks with a strong voice and asked about their day. Did they realize he was a dying man? I don't think so.

Marv held the first bottle of contrast and took one sip at a time. After each sip, he drifted off, and I'd catch the bottle as he lost his grip. I'd wake him, "Honey, another sip," over and over until, finally, he got the two bottles down.

He was no sooner finished when the tech came. The tech was not as friendly as all the folks we'd already encountered. All business, he stood in the doorway and called Marv's name. We got up, and I walked alongside Marv as he swayed after the tech down the hall.

I stood outside the door and waited. When he came out, still carrying his empty prep bottles, he said in an out-of-breath, gravelly voice, "I could hardly do it." I asked, "What?" He said, "Get my legs, my body, up on the table."

My mind went into movie mode. I could picture him trying, probably without any help from the all-business tech, to lift his legs on and off the table. Helplessness hit again. I was trying to be there for Marv every step of the way, and I had messed up once more. I wondered why I hadn't insisted on going into the room with him, at least until he was on the table. I knew why, of course; I was not operating at full speed myself.

I texted Kath that we were finished and ready for pickup. She was parked with the kids, whom she'd picked up from camp, nearby. As Kath rounded a corner into my sight, I felt my tension lessen with the prospect of help. I helped Marv again into her vehicle. His legs were dead weight.

And, as if we'd only taken a trip to his favorite Menards, there was Marv, booming to the kids, "How was your day at camp?"

I'd always known Marv was strong. But to see him acting normal when he was extraordinarily compromised is a memory that will always stay with me.

When we arrived home, a package was waiting from my sister Rose and her daughters. Kath took a picture of us, Marv in his lawn chair, me standing next to him with the opened box of goodies. Marv looks pained in his face; his cigarette dangles from his right hand. There is the smell of the lilac bush and the occasional sound of tweeting birds, but nothing else was normal at the time of this last photo of the two of us.

The kids were playing inside; Marv, Kath, and I were outside. I wondered aloud, "I hope we don't have to wait until tomorrow to get the results." While we brainstormed about what to have for dinner, my phone rang. I raced inside to pick up the call.

It was the hospice doctor, with the results. Marv was full of cancer. The doctor gave details about the cancer's extensive involvement in the abdomen. No wonder Marv was in such terrible pain.

"The disease is coming to a head," he said. "At this point, most people come into hospice, but I understand from the nurses here that Marv wants to die at home."

I said, "Yes." I knew Kathleen or Jon would drop everything to be with me 24/7 if I needed help. The referrals hospice had given me at the beginning were an option too.

And then he asked a question that will forever stay in my mind: "Are you up for this?"

Of course I was. Hadn't I promised Marv he would die at home? True, I wasn't at all in touch with how fatigued I was. When I said yes, he asked, "Are you sure?" I answered again—yes.

He then said if I had paper and pen, he'd give me instructions. I scribbled into my little notebook the names of the medications, the dosages, and the times I could administer them.

About a half hour later, I asked the doctor if he would talk to Marv. I brought my phone outside to him and watched as Marv listened intently for a few minutes. He nodded his head and said an "uh huh" a few times, then quickly assumed a normal, jovial voice. He even asked the doctor to insert a pipe for his backed-up bowels, like they used to do for bloated cattle on the farm, and promised he'd smile for him just like the cattle used to with the resulting relief. I marveled at his continued fortitude.

I don't recall any heavy-duty conversation with Marv after that call. No "this is it" kind of thing. The kids were playing in the house. To get out of the sun; the three of us, along with Michael who'd joined us, moved to the garage. It was a warm, quiet evening. Marv said he still had financial information to tell us; Michael thought to record it. Nothing new—more about RMDs, dividends, and future budgets—but it affirmed Marv's intention that I would have no financial worries.

After Madison had given Marv his meds, the kids left. A couple friends I'd made through OLLI stopped in. They wanted to pick up a copy of Marv's book. The guy noted Marv's discomfort trying to move a tad in the lawn chair. He jumped up. "Can I help you, Marv?" Marv said, "No, I'm all right."

A neighbor peeked under the half-open garage door. His wife had dropped in a bit earlier and heard our news. He came to say goodbye and asked, "Marv, I've never known. What kind of work did you do?"

Marv launched into a twenty-minute account of his business, why he'd started it, the importance of access to health care for all kids, and what still needs to be done. He had little eye contact and stopped to take a breath every few words, but otherwise, his tone was as firm and fervent as always when he talked about his work.

Ironically, living with Marv's passion for his life's work for so many years, I used to joke Marv would die advocating for children's access to health care. As it turned out, except for a few more sentences, those words to our neighbor were his final ones.

After our guests had left, Marv stayed outside until after ten. He was floating in and out, losing focus. Once, while I sat with him, he slowly moved his head to stare at me. We locked eyes. From way down deep, he murmured while catching his breath, "Our remaining days would look like . . . love and caring."

I hovered alongside as he undressed for bed in the closet. When he stood by the sink, I stayed next to him, ready to brace a fall. He elbowed me away. "I can do it myself."

My cheeks felt as though they might shatter from repressed tears. I'd always known the end goal for a nurse with a dying patient was to help the patient die with dignity, and now Marv was showing me how he wanted to maintain his dignity until the end.

We swayed, one small step at a time, to his side of the bed. He fell halfway onto the bed at an angle and whispered, "Rest." I understood he needed to rest before we got him straightened out. I said, "Let's pray now then, honey, while you rest." I waited for him to start, as he'd always done these last seven months. His eyes were closed. He was panting from the exhaustion of getting undressed and into bed.

When I could see he was not going to start praying, I said, "I'll pray tonight, honey." Again, I don't know why I had my phone on me or what prompted me to think of recording the prayer. But I must have known this may be our last communication, his last words.

So I started, "Our heavenly Father, we thank you for our life together. We thank you for the many blessings we've had all these years.

"We pray for you now to help Marv enter your kingdom without pain. We've learned today of extensive metastasis of his cancer, and we were expecting this, so it's not a surprise, and we just want the transition to your heavenly home to be without pain.

"We thank you for the doctors and the nurses at Avera for helping us, being with us, walking with us every step of the way.

"We thank you for giving us since January—it's now almost the end of July—to have this time together to travel, to live intentionally, to have many close, love-making sessions, to have Marv bragging to everybody it's been the best six or seven months of our lives.

"Be with us now as we rest. Help us to wake up with some clarity of mind and some sense of peace about facing our final days."

Then I ended with, "Would you like to add anything, honey?"

Marv joined in, voice raspy, gasping between phrases, "Help us to just finish out, without pain . . . discomfort . . . to transition . . ."

After about fifteen seconds, I closed our prayer: "Thank you, Lord. You've heard Marv's wishes. We know you are an all-loving God. We know you have watched over us through this whole journey of Marv's cancer.

"For Jesus's sake, amen."

Marv struggled to get straight on the bed. With eyes closed, he turned to kiss me two or three times. Exhaling in pain, he drifted off. I hoped he'd sleep. After all the meds I'd given him, some doctor-ordered, some by his request, I hoped his pain was lessened.

I still hadn't absorbed the finality of our situation. Too tired to take one more step, I flopped on the bed, snuggled on my stomach next to Marv, and placed my hand on his chest. My breathing synced with his. At long last, there was no evidence of pain.

Words from Marv

I've had a full life. I have been richly blessed, and I'm ready.

Tuesday, July 24, 2018

Notes

At 5:30 a.m., Marv jarred slightly as he coughed. I started his scheduled doses of morphine for pain and Ativan for restlessness. Waiting for his involuntary swallows so I could drop the medication into the inside of his cheek, I sensed he could hear me but did not have the strength to respond. I looked at his face: no lines, no grimace. No evidence of pain.

With enormous relief, I left him and went to our kitchen table to jot notes in my little book. I'd purchased some piano hymn CDs for these last hours and put them on. "Shall We Gather at the River" came on first. I sat at the table, weeping. The time had come. I wrote, "Oh my, oh my, oh my. His pain is almost gone."

Kathleen came at eight. She moved the CD player from the living room to Marv's bedside. The rest of the day blurs in the movie of my mind. I stopped writing notes except for charting the meds. He stayed comfortable and at peace with no labored breathing; he never required oxygen.

Our pastor came for two hours in the afternoon. Michael had joined us, and the four of us stood around our bar talking. We went to Marv's bedside for the pastor to pray. I told Marv, with a louder voice than I'd been using, that Pastor David was here. Marv was on his side, facing the door. I knew he heard me because his forehead wrinkled, and his eyes cracked open for a second. This was another result of the sedating meds, but it was reassuring to have evidence that he could hear Pastor David's final prayer, spoken in the pastor's usual manner, as one friend has described it, of "quiet grace."

After the pastor left, we sat around, in and out of Marv's room, and neighbors came bringing food. We had two sets of donuts, one from a popular bakery in town and the other from a grocery store. In our condition, which I can only describe as barely functioning and beyond fatigue, we conducted a taste test to decide which donuts were better. We cut them into thirds and ate from both boxes: Boston cream, chocolate frosted, assorted Long Johns. In between, to cleanse our palettes, we sampled from a box of assorted homemade cookies brought over by a neighbor. We ate nothing nutritious all afternoon. With their larger size and lower cost, the donuts from the grocery store won.

After Michael left to pick up the kids from where they were staying and to take them home, Kath and I spent several hours on Marv's bed. We talked with him, sang hymns along with the CDs ("It Is Well with My Soul," "Jesus Loves Me," and "Jesus Saves") and read Scriptures: Psalm 23, Psalm 90, Psalm 121. There was no response. No eyelid flicker. No squeezing of the hand. No groaning in pain. As the evening wore on, Kath had a newspaper and started reading some of the ads. As only she could do, she joshed with Marv that there were good sales and that he could go shopping with us. She knew he hated our kind of shopping. Whenever she invited him along, he'd look at her, exasperated, and say, "Get going. Leave me alone, will you?" So, after some lighthearted chatter, Kath assured Marv he could go whenever he was ready; she and her brother would make sure to take care of me.

Kathleen went to sleep in our guest room. I fell into bed, spooned behind Marv; I still didn't grasp that these were possibly the final hours. He was breathing comfortably, no panting, no gasping, no shallow irregular rhythm. His body was warm. It could have been like any other night.

PART VI

TRANSITIONS

CHAPTER TWENTY-TWO

Wednesday, July 25, 2018

Notes

I awoke with a start around four, still spooned behind Marv, sensing something was off. Could this be it? Just that fast, I became aware that my left arm around his chest was not moving. Instinctively, I started to count. One . . . two . . . three . . .

On the count of twelve, Marv took one deep, noisy breath and exhaled.

For the last time. "In the twinkling of an eye . . ."

I checked his pulse. None. I bounded out of bed down the hall and opened Kath's door. She bolted up: "He's gone, isn't he?"

We ran back to the bedroom. I don't remember in what order we did things next. I know we cried. A lot. Took pictures of our hands over his. Once, Kath wondered if he were still breathing; I took out my stethoscope and listened. Nothing. I know Kath called Jon, who was vacationing with Sheri in Iceland. He'd been on his way down to breakfast in the hotel when he'd hesitated by the door to his room. Grace, again.

I know Kath asked me to make the decision when to call hospice. I told her I wanted to clean Dad up a bit first. She said, "Hospice will do that, Mom."

And I remember saying, "No, it's the last thing I can do for Dad."

A few minutes later, I called hospice for the final time. Nurse Mary came, the same nurse I'd talked to the prior night. She'd offered to stay the night with me before she knew Kath was here. Now, she offered to do a liturgy consisting of Bible readings and prayers that commemorated Marv's life and entrusted him to God's care. It had three speaking parts. We stood next to Marv's body on the bed and read our parts. It was one of the most holy times of my life, the most sacred of times—a time when I felt deeply that Marv's soul, his essence, had gone to heaven, and what remained was merely his soul's earthly container.

From then on until dinnertime—about twelve hours—every moment was filled with something we had to do or a phone call we had to make. When we were ready, Mary called the funeral home. When the transporter arrived, I asked if I could take pictures. I explained our son was in Iceland, and I wanted him to be a part of this. No problem. I followed the worker from his vehicle, a long black van with blackened windows, through the front door, down the long hallway to the bedroom, and back. As he drove away, I took a photo to memorialize Marv leaving our home for the last time.

Kath and I had dressed before Mary came. I remember having no feeling—or maybe it was a feeling I wouldn't know how to describe, perhaps a combination of weary, empty, and wired. By two in the afternoon, I'd tracked down and notified Marv's eight siblings or their spouses and my two. Kath had made her calls. And we went to the funeral home to do whatever we had to do there. Since we'd made prior arrangements, I thought we only had to plan their part in the service. But then the funeral director, Jane, asked me what I wanted to serve at the luncheon. I didn't know that was their task; I thought I'd plan the lunch with church staff. My mind blanked. With a quizzical expression on my face, I said, "Toothpicks and water?" She must have been used to folks like me because she laughed. She offered to give me the options, from least expensive to most. When she arrived up the ladder to roast beef and mashed potatoes, I blurted, "That's it. That's the traditional Dutch Sunday dinner we both had as kids."

When we were finished, Kath asked, "Where's my dad now?" Jane answered, "Mr. Roelofs is in our care. Would you like to see him?" At the same time, Kath said yes and I said no. I looked at her and said, "Okay."

I heard the gurney rumbling down the hall. Jane ushered us into a small room where Marv lay under a homemade quilt. I felt the same disassociated feeling, that the "who" I was seeing was simply what had been the earthly container of Marv's soul. I remembered being present at the deaths of patients during my practice years and family members crying over the bodies of their loved ones. I felt no need to cry. I was more curious about what they had done to make sure Marv's eyes and mouth stayed shut. I'd had to tape eyelids and put washcloth rolls under chins when we'd waited for orderlies to bring bodies down to the autopsy room.

Maybe it was being a nurse that made me feel so clinical; I don't know. I caressed Marv's face and took one long, last look, sealing into memory his hairline, closed eyes, nose, closed mouth, and chin. Kath took a photo of the two of us. I look like the mourner I was—weary, broken, wearing a white tunic-length blouse with a stand-up collar, trying tenderly to say goodbye but not knowing how.

That evening, because we had tickets and because we were too wired to relax, Michael, Kathleen, and I went to see a local production of the play, *Tuesdays with Morrie*. When we were walking out, Kath turned to me: "What are you going to miss most about Dad?" I knew. "His listening." I thought of the play. Morrie thrived on having a listener; I would no longer have mine.

Obituary

ROELOFS, MARVIN D.

Marv Roelofs, 77, passed away at home in Sioux Falls, South Dakota, on July 25, 2018, from Stage IV small cell lung cancer. After refusing chemotherapy upon diagnosis in January, his parting words the past few months typified his faith: "I've had a full life. I've been richly blessed, and I'm ready to go." Always a "can do" type of man, his favorite phrases illustrated his optimistic philosophy: "I don't like being told I can't do something." "There is no such word as can't." "My approach is to challenge and go beyond whatever is happening."

Mr. Roelofs was born on March 21, 1941, and raised on a farm outside of Prinsburg, Minnesota. In 1959, he left to attend Calvin College in Grand Rapids, Michigan. In 1962, he married Lois (Hoitenga), whom he'd met the first day at Calvin, and in 1966, they moved to the Chicago area where he graduated from Jane Addams School of Social Work. After fifty years in Chicago, they moved to Sioux Falls in 2016 to be near their daughter and her family.

Marv's life passion centered on his belief that every child with disabilities is unique and needs opportunities to develop their potential. As an advocate for the provision of health care services to children in the public-school system, he created TAMES Health Resource Service Management to enable public schools to access federal dollars to share in the cost of the health care services. In over thirty years of operation, TAMES has generated in excess of $270 million for the public-school districts in Illinois.

As a farm-raised boy living in the city as an adult, Marv brought many make-it and fix-it skills with him. He especially enjoyed gardening, mowing lawn on a zero-turn John Deere, and making what he called "Marv's Functional Furniture," including a host of end tables, study desks, and bookshelves for Lois and play equipment for their children and grandchildren (even a club house on top of a swing set). Other interests involved managing the couple's investments and serving in their churches as deacon, elder, and trustee and giving children's sermons.

He is survived by his wife, Lois; son, Jon (Sheri) Roelofs, of Kent, Washington; daughter, Kathleen (Michael) Ridder, of Sioux Falls, South Dakota; and grandchildren Kristin (Allan) Jensen, Kyle Roelofs (fiancée Kaileen Runia), and Megan Roelofs (fiancé Shane Benner), and Madison Ridder and Jacob Ridder.

Mr. Roelofs is also survived by sisters Marcella Ulferts Sportel; Joan Ulferts (Melvin); Shirley Diemer (Harm); and Linda Diemer (Ev); brothers Rev. Curt (Phyllis) and Roger (Marilyn); and sisters-in-law Cynthia Roelofs and Arlet Roelofs. He is preceded in death by his parents, Mr. Lou and Mrs. Anna Roelofs; brothers Rev. Harlan and Harry; and brothers-in-law Walter Ulferts and George Sportel.

A Celebration of Life service will be held Saturday, August 11, at 11:00 a.m. at Westminster Presbyterian Church, 3801 E. 26th Street, Sioux Falls.

In lieu of flowers, contributions may be made to Avera@Home Hospice Sioux Falls or TANA (Trinity Alumni Nurses Association) at Trinity Christian College, 6601 West College Drive, Palos Heights, Illinois, 60463.

Marianna's Blog: "Marv Roelofs and Apple Sauce"

From NursingStories.org, dated August 1, 2018

"Making applesauce sort of represents living life to the fullest. I think prayer is sometimes about asking God to let us do what we can and enjoy ourselves. Picking apples and making applesauce has made me do that."—Marv Roelofs

I called Marv soon after he received the diagnosis of Stage IV small cell lung cancer this past January. I don't recall if I have ever called him in all the 40-plus years his wife, Lois, and I have been friends. Now in the past few months, I had called him twice.

After his diagnosis, there was a sense of urgency. The doctors had told him the cancer was very aggressive, so when Marv declined treatment, I figured I better talk to him right away. How long would he be around? I needed to tell him how I appreciated his encouragement and support of my friendship with Lois.

Lois and I met in Chicago. We were two nurses with two young children each—a boy and a girl—and both ready to break out of the stay-at-home-mom mode. Together, in the late '70s and early '80s, we completed undergraduate and graduate nursing degrees. In 1992, I moved from Chicago.

We didn't need to get permission from our husbands to spend time away from home or to spend money on plane tickets when we rendezvoused over the years. But it was Marv's encouragement and support of our long-distance friendship and warm reception and hospitality during my visits that I wanted to acknowledge. Since Lois didn't cook, or wash dishes for that matter, it was Marv who made the dinners, baked the banana bread, and served Lois and me as we continued deep into our conversation—as women are inclined to do.

My phone call to him now melted into tears for both of us. Maybe the rawness of Marv's diagnosis and the awareness of impending death were too close to the surface. I was glad I had called to say thank you.

After that first phone call and when Marv didn't die in a matter of days or weeks, as the doctors had suggested, I called him a second time. It was about six months after the first phone call. He had written a book of his life and made fifty-five copies to pass along to family and friends. I read it almost all in one evening. I knew some of Marv's stories already, but his life on the farm and the details of his self-started business were new to me. I was especially taken with the way he wrote—as if we were sitting in his living room in Sioux Falls, or back in Chicago, just sharing his recollections.

That second phone call was more uplifting. We laughed more. Cried less. I told him how much I liked the book, especially the story about him making applesauce.

The first fall after Marv and Lois moved from Chicago to Sioux Falls, he noticed that many people didn't pick the apples from their trees. The apples just fell and rotted on the ground. He knocked on doors asking to harvest the apples, not for profit, but to donate them to the homeless and churches and to make applesauce.

It was right around apple-picking season that I visited Lois and Marv in Sioux Falls. With a refrigerator and freezer stuffed with applesauce in Ziploc bags, Marv sent Lois and me into the neighborhood to give away the first samplings of his culinary concoction to neighbors whom Marv and Lois had barely met. The friendly neighbors graciously accepted our offering.

Marv was a successful businessperson, a loving husband, dad, and grandfather. Like all of us, he was also a complicated human. But it was Marv, the person who picked the apples and made applesauce, whose memory is the warmest in my heart.

Marv died at 4:10 a.m. on July 25.

CHAPTER TWENTY-THREE

Thursday, July 26, 2018

Notes

The day after. Drifting awake at seven, I smelled the lingering scent of lavender from the diffuser that a mutual friend of ours had sent for its calming effect. The aroma eased me into awareness that Marv was no longer here. My hand instinctively swept over the bed beside me. Flat. Empty. Deserted. There was no sound of Marv's breath, only the faint whirring of the ceiling fan. The morning sun, peeking through the slanted blinds, created a warm glimmer of hope across the room.

Clutching Marv's pillow, I let my mind travel. *I'm a widow now. Hate the word. Will have to think up something better. What do I need to do first? What am I missing?*

Then I remembered something was on my schedule. I'd signed up months earlier for a local aging conference, anticipating I would have been alone for some time by now. *Should I go? Is it too soon to go out in public by myself? What if I run into someone I know? Am I rested enough? Will I faint from accumulated fatigue? Will buried tears be unearthed by a trigger? Will I embarrass myself?*

After I'd gotten up and while I was drinking my protein and blueberry breakfast shake, I remembered that I'd seen another woman from my church at this same event the prior year, when I'd gone alone. On the chance she might be going again, I called her and dove right in. I hoped she'd remember me because we were still fairly new to the area. I hoped she'd heard my announcement at church the previous Sunday about Marv's change. I hoped she wouldn't think I was off the wall with my request.

I rambled on: "My husband just died yesterday, but I have a ticket to the aging conference, and I saw you there last year and wondered if you were going. I'm feeling okay now, but I don't trust myself and may need someone to prop me up."

After a pause where she was probably digesting my spill of words, she extended condolences and then said, "Funny you should call. I do have a ticket, but I just decided I wouldn't go because I have no one to go with. But I'd love to go with you. And prop you up, if necessary. Meet you in the lobby at quarter to nine."

Grace? Of course.

I roamed the house, taking stock of the never-used wheelchair in the foyer awaiting pickup by hospice and the commode, used only as a table for the CD player, that hospice would not take back. The silence reverberating through the house gave me the jitters. *Or is it my nerves not knowing how to react to the loss of the need to be vigilant?* Feeling like a windup toy ready to spin off a table, I was glad I had some place to go.

I showered and dressed and was on my way by half past eight to the auditorium where the conference was held. The woman and I met in the lobby as planned. After a warm hug, we walked together into a large room that held round tables set up to seat eight; most tables were filled. There was just time to smile at our tablemates before the speaker was introduced.

As I'd hoped, the conference was made for me that day. The speaker, Sister Joyce Rupp, spoke on "Liberating the Heart: Spirituality of Elderhood." From habit, I jotted down a few pages of notes: "Who teaches us how to grow old? Who helps us? Who encourages us?" *Yes, who can I depend on now that I am alone?*

Oftentimes quoting others, Rupp made it seem like she was speaking only to me. "Be at home with yourself—love who you are." *Okay, so it's all right that I am here the day after my husband died.* "Elderhood is a time of letting go, a 'crossing over' stage in life." *True. Who am I now after "letting go" of my marriage? Without Marv in my life?* "You have to trust God." *Yes—exactly what my older sister Rose had told me when I was thinking about retiring early.* "Don't allow yourself to congeal. Be open to possibility." *Exactly what Marv had said: "I'm the one who's dying. Not you."*

Rupp even mentioned Atul Gawande's *Being Mortal* and the idea that the needs of people will differ. *How true. Bucking a norm, Marv had chosen no chemo.*

The conference finished at 2:30 p.m. I held myself together, soaking in the always comforting and sometimes humorous words of the speaker. I bought a few books on grief, complimented a woman in the lunch line on her red strappy sandals, and thanked my church friend for being an all-purpose-whatever-I-needed support for me throughout the day.

That evening, after I'd eaten heated-up leftovers, I thought I'd better write down every detail of Marv's passing before I forgot. I retreated to my study and typed up a final blog post, giving a play-by-play of the prior few days.

I was finally alone, and the house was quiet. Writing, I've always known, is a way of processing for me. After every word was down, I felt lighter, like I'd unearthed layers of information and emotion on the page. I could breathe easier. I felt at peace, knowing I'd completed my task of fulfilling Marv's wish to die at home. The responsibility I'd taken on was finished. And I was enormously happy that I managed to hang in. The feeling was like my graduations, marching down the aisles for my degrees in nursing to the tune of "Pomp and Circumstance" with that joyous feeling that all the work I'd done had paid off.

I wondered what Marv would say about this finale to the story I'd started seven months earlier. I realized I would never again read my posts to him. I imagined his approval—though, he would probably have added, "We did it, honey. Together. We made it happen for me to live out my life like I wanted." I pictured a smile and a peaceful look on his face.

Lying in bed that night, I felt as though someone had lifted a weighted blanket off my body. My mind wandered in gratitude, recalling all the good things of these past few months: Marv accepting his diagnosis. Holding to his decision for no treatment, unwavering. Requesting hospice right away. Preparing end-of-life legal and financial paperwork. Assuring me, "You'll do fine." Urging me to continue my interests of writing, traveling, and taking classes.

Throughout, he naturally embodied his belief that if this was God's time for him, he was ready to go home. I was thankful, too, that I'd made it even though I'd come close to the edge. It felt like Marv must have sensed I was at my breaking point and decided to pass away right at that time.

Now ready to sleep, I turned on my side, pretending to mold myself behind him. Patting his pillow, I started a new nighttime ritual of praying alone and whispering, "Night, honey. Love you."

CHAPTER TWENTY-FOUR

November 18, 2018

"Are you 'Louise'?" the tall man shouted above the packed crowd of people catapulting forward at Ben Gurion airport in Tel Aviv.

I was so relieved that I was ready to answer to anything vaguely sounding like Lois. "Yes," I shouted back and waved my hand.

Six weeks after Marv's death, an unsolicited email had arrived from the educational travel program company Road Scholar, announcing a trip to Israel and Jordan in two months' time. Instantly, I wanted to go. The timing felt perfect; I would visit places where Jesus lived on earth the same year that Marv went to heaven. I reasoned that a trip so soon would give me a deadline for plowing through the after-death paperwork. Marv had never wanted to go but I'd been interested, so I welcomed the email as a sign that I was supposed to go. Besides, he'd told me over and over to take as many classes and trips as I wanted. So why not?

In the prior six weeks, I'd proven to myself that I could survive, physically at least, without him. The biggest thing, of course, was cooking. I still hadn't gotten interested in the kitchen, so a protein shake for breakfast, cottage cheese with cantaloupe for lunch, and a bagged salad and a meat patty for dinner had become my staples. If I didn't know something house-wise, I hounded my kids, neighbors, or friends for help.

When I called Kathleen about going to the Middle East, she said, "You can rationalize anything." Probably true. I could hear the unsaid "sheesh" in her voice as if to say, "What next?" When I called Jon, I could feel his approving shrug on the phone: "Go for it."

I signed up.

When the time came, I flew to Chicago a day early to get my flight to Munich/Tel Aviv and stayed overnight at the O'Hare Hilton. Unlike some folks who don't know O'Hare Airport well, having lived in Chicago I was familiar with and loved the ambience of its multitudes of travelers and terminals.

Following Marv's own edict in the last few years that he'd always travel business class ("I've worked hard; I've earned it"), I settled into my reclining seat for the eight-and-a-half-hour flight to Munich, feeling pretty smug, as if I were a world traveler. Arriving in Munich half asleep, I slung my backpack on my back, marched like a woman with a purpose, and scooted through checkpoints and corridors some forty gates till I found the one for Tel Aviv. Sweating up a storm, I made it just in time to board the final, nearly five-hour leg of my journey.

I arrived in Tel Aviv dead tired to a horribly packed and chaotic airport. But there was my Road Scholar contact faithfully waiting for me, searching for "Louise." I shot my hand into the air and swung it back and forth, screaming, "Road Scholar? Road Scholar?"

Relief. My pulse was pounding at a rate of about 120 in my chest. He signaled for me to follow him, and I was ready to follow anybody in this swarming sea of strangers. I pushed my way through the masses and stuck close behind him until we got out of the building.

But then, standing on the curb alongside a plethora of blinding headlights (it was now dark) from dozens of taxis, the man pointed to a taxi about four cars to the left from where I was standing.

I followed his pointed finger. He stayed behind.

Well, I thought, *here goes nothing. I'm a new widow in a new big city, knowing no one, trapped in a beyond-weary body, operating on fumes only. But I've always loved adventures, right? Well, this is one.*

As I walked forward, the driver in the designated taxi leaned toward me. When I reached the car, I opened the back door. *Am I really getting into this cab with a strange man in a strange city?*

The driver smiled and asked, "Are you Louise?"

"Yes," I said gladly. *Sure.* "I'm Louise."

He held up a piece of paper for me to read in the dim light of the cab. There it was: my name, Lois Roelofs.

I settled back into my seat and inhaled several times. *I'm in Tel Aviv.*

My driver, it turned out, was alarmingly handsome. Dark curly hair. Dark swarthy complexion. An amiable smile. An appealing accented English. *Am I really safe with this man? Is he always this charming, or am I just too tired to be rational?*

During the one-hour drive to the Jerusalem hotel where I would meet up with other Road Scholars, he swerved at roller-coaster speed between multiple lanes, up and down hills, and around a lot of curves. As if to put me at ease, he said, "You have to know how to drive here. No one watches speed limits or stays in their lane."

My eyes caught only a blur of racing red taillights in the dead of night. I felt as though I were in a dream. I sat back in my seat, prayed for safety, and giggled to myself. *I've done it. I've gotten here. And I'm on my way to Jerusalem. All by myself.*

EPILOGUE

Before I say farewell, I want to say a few things that I hope will be helpful to you, so pretend we're sipping mochas together and read along.

Losses are huge when one becomes a widow. Mine, I think, were particularly distressing because, as you know already, Marv did everything around the house. I can't count the times I complained, half-joking, "I didn't sign up for this!" But those tasks can be learned. What can't be learned is how you will deal with the simple absence of your loved one.

Early on in my life as a widow, my older sister Rose, a widow of eleven years, told me, "It's the absence of his presence that I miss." She nailed it. Especially if you have no others living with you, it can get awfully quiet and lonely. You have no one who will ask you how you're feeling. No one to ask you what you've planned for the day or how your day went. No one for whom you are number one in their life anymore.

A few months after Marv's passing, I ran into an older pastor whose wife had passed away the year before. He said a similar thing as my sister: "It's the loss of someone to do nothing with that I miss most." That's a profound statement in its simplicity. In other words, it means there's no one to just hang out with you. Marv's recliner now sits empty.

So, how have I dealt with this inevitable sense of loss? Probably like anyone whose husband tells her that after he's gone she should "live high on the hog": I've taken classes, stayed active with OLLI, traveled, and served as an elder in the church. And I've done some redecorating that we'd planned before Marv became ill. I still monitor my activity level to prevent fibromyalgia flares. I continue to actively write for my blog as well.

Naturally, my life alone is very different from my life with Marv, but if I can get out of bed, learn something new, spend time with family and friends, and not have the house blow up or the car break down, I'm carrying on exactly as Marv wished me to do.

But about the real work of grieving. The weeping. The loneliness. The absence of my best confidant.

Yes, I've wept. But I've found I'm not a crier. I've wept uncontrollably a few times, but not as often as I'd thought I might.

As far as loneliness? Other widows have told me that for them, evenings are the worst. But Marv always went to bed at nine, and I was up until at least eleven. I was used to spending the later evening alone. Still, there's a void in the time from six to nine when, after Marv had served me dinner, we'd spend an hour or more processing each of our days.

I wish I could say that lack of having a listener hurts less as time passes. I can't. Every day things pop up I want to tell Marv. I talk instead to his cremains in a silver vase on the floor-to-ceiling bookshelf he built in our living room. I read. Write. Watch PBS. Call a friend. Play the piano.

And the time after I go to bed? There are no words, other than "grievous," to describe not being able to spoon behind Marv. The loss of warmth, the loss of closeness, the loss of lovemaking. Instead, I continue to tap Marv's pillow and pray.

But still I'm living the life he wished for me. As he said to me in his final days, "I'm the one who's dying. Not you. Remember that as you go forward."

Finally, I'm grateful for the continuous evidence of God's grace that supported me from Marv's diagnosis, through the months of dying, and then death. I'm happy that early on I learned all I could about his illness and involved all my support systems. And now I'm happy I've completed this book as he wished. What will I do in the future? For sure, I'll continue writing. Maybe another book, expanding on the summary above of my first years without him.

I'm open to whatever happens; maybe I'll get a sign.

After his passing, Marv showed up once when I was serving communion at my church for the first time. I'd helped serve the bread and was waiting on the pulpit to bring the juice to those in the pews, and I vowed to concentrate on the moment—on the honor and privilege, at long last as a woman, to serve communion.

While I was focusing on the pastor's face, his words, and his pouring of the juice, I became aware of an image of Marv, wearing his brown, white, and rust textured sweater, hovering high over the pastor's right shoulder. On his face, there was a look of solemnity, as if to say he showed up to support me in my new role. I blinked and he was still there; I blinked once more and he was gone.

Maybe he'll show up again, next time with a grin and a comment, "Looks like you're doing fine. I told you so." I'll just smile and say, "I heard you, honey. I'm trying."

ACKNOWLEDGMENTS

Writing this book on a personal and painful topic was made possible by support from others to whom I'm thankful to God for putting into my life at such a crucial time and for whom I will always be grateful. My thanks go to:

Sandra Scofield for accepting me into her two-week intensive memoir class at the Iowa Summer Writing Festival and, as my first editor, giving me the encouragement to continue.

Beta readers Lois Barliant, Linda Keane, Kay Hoitenga, Amy Nagelkirk, Cindy Schlimgen, and Carol Slater. These women told me exactly how my story hit them and gave me what I needed to continue the process of revision.

Laura Matthews, developmental editor, who helped me shape my collection of notes, emails, blog posts, and memories into a cohesive narrative arc.

Andy Carmichael, publisher at Deep River Books; and the Deep River team—including Tamara Barnet (editorial and design management), Carl Simmons (editing), Carolyn Currey (proofreading), and Robin Black (cover design)—for their prompt, detailed, and sensitive attention to my book. It was a privilege to entrust DRB once again with a book of mine.

Fellow Chicago transplants to Sioux Falls, Catherine Lacey and Carol Slater, for weekly in-person (or Zoom during the epidemic) support. We discovered that their love for making puzzles is like my love for writing a book—lots of pieces and patience required.

My forever friend and fellow nurse/author/blogger, Marianna Crane, for weekly calls and sporadic visits over many years to brainstorm life—connections that I especially appreciated during Marv's diagnosis-to-death trajectory and the writing of this book. Everyone should have such a loyal friend who understands what you're saying between the lines.

My always thoughtful and dependable kids: my son and his spouse, Jon and Sheri Roosendaal Roelofs, and my daughter and her spouse, Kathleen and Michael Ridder, for supporting me through the care of their dad. It truly does take a village. And lots of love to my eight grandchildren: Kristin and Allan Jensen, Kyle and Kaileen Runia Roelofs, Megan and Shane Benner, Madison Ridder, and Jacob Ridder for the various ways they let me and their grandpa know that he mattered.

Lastly, a loving thanks to Marv, who wanted our story told, and for emphatically believing I would make it happen. I hope and pray our experience may be of help in some way to you or someone you love.

ABOUT THE AUTHOR

 Lois Roelofs holds a PhD in Nursing Science. After retirement in 2000 as Professor Emerita of Nursing at Trinity Christian College, she plunged immediately into her long-time interest in writing nonfiction, initially inspired by Anne Lamott and Natalie Goldberg. Continuing her love for learning, she completed the four-year University of Chicago Basic Program of Liberal Education and has completed more than thirty writing workshops. In her first book, *Caring Lessons: A Nursing Professor's Journey of Faith and Self* (Deep River, 2010), she told the story of her forty-year nursing career. After fifty years of living in Chicago, she now resides in South Dakota near her daughter's family and shares a winter home in Arizona with her son's family; at both places, Lois can enjoy her mochas, the dubious fun of aging, and chats with kids and grandkids. Follow her blog at loisroelofs.com.

Printed in the United States
by Baker & Taylor Publisher Services